# The Wisdom of Ralph Waldo Emerson:

# Nature, Self-Reliance, and the Oversoul

ISBN: 9798263787844

# Chapters

## The Sage of Concord and the Voice of the New World

The story of Ralph Waldo Emerson begins not merely with a man, but with a voice — a voice that sought to speak for a new people, in a new world, at a time when the cultural air was still thick with the remnants of Old Europe. In the small New England town of Concord, among orchards, narrow lanes, and quiet meadows, a thinker arose who dared to declare that the sacred could be found not only in Scripture but in the trees and rivers; not only in inherited traditions, but in the immediacy of one's own heart. Emerson did not wish to construct a system of philosophy in the scholastic sense, nor did he aspire to found a church with dogma and creeds. His was a different mission: to awaken. To awaken men and women to the living divinity present in nature and in themselves. To call forth in each soul the recognition that, as he wrote, "the currents of the Universal Being circulate through me; I am part or particle of God."

The nineteenth century was young when Emerson entered it, born in Boston in 1803 into a lineage of ministers, preachers, and teachers. New England's stern Puritan heritage still shadowed its people, a heritage of rigorous faith and discipline, yet also of inward searching. Emerson inherited that legacy, but from the start there was in him a restlessness, a sense that the old forms were no longer adequate. He would spend his life seeking a language to articulate the grandeur of spirit that he felt coursing beneath the surface of things, a language capable of lifting the minds of his contemporaries from the inherited chains of tradition into a more spacious realm.

Emerson's task was not solitary, though his temperament inclined toward solitude. He was surrounded by a circle of seekers, thinkers, reformers, and poets who together gave shape to what would be called **Transcendentalism** — a word both elusive and radiant. It signified, at its heart, the conviction that truth cannot be confined to institutions or books alone, but must be lived and directly experienced. The Transcendentalist movement was the first great intellectual flowering of the United States, and Emerson was its clear center. His essays, sermons, lectures, and journals became both manifesto and scripture for a generation that yearned to step beyond the inherited authority of Europe and into its own spiritual independence.

It is impossible to understand Emerson without understanding his America. The nation itself was in its youth, scarcely six decades from the

Declaration of Independence. A vast continent stretched westward, rivers uncharted, mountains unnamed, possibilities untested. The air was thick with the optimism of a people who felt themselves destined to shape a civilization unlike any before. And yet, with that optimism came doubt, the shadows of slavery, the displacement of indigenous peoples, the struggles of industrialization, and the ever-present tension between inherited European culture and the untamed land. Emerson gave to this young America a philosophy equal to its vastness. He declared that the divine was not confined to the old cathedrals of Europe, but revealed itself in the pines of New England, in the sudden rush of a brook, in the courage of a mind willing to stand alone.

His life was marked by both tragedy and transformation. The early death of his father left him in the care of a determined mother and a line of schoolmasters. The loss of his first wife, Ellen, just two years after their marriage, would plunge him into despair so deep that he questioned the very foundations of his faith and vocation. Yet from that loss he emerged with a new vision, one that would eventually carry him beyond the pulpit into a vocation broader and freer: that of the essayist, lecturer, and sage. His journeys to

Europe brought him into conversation with Coleridge, Wordsworth, and Carlyle, encounters that nourished but also tested his independence. From Carlyle in particular he drew both inspiration and a lasting friendship, but always with the insistence that the American mind must speak in its own accent, must not merely echo the tones of the Old World.

When Emerson spoke of **Nature**, he was not describing scenery or pastoral charm. He was invoking a living presence, a vast book of revelation written in rivers and skies. He called his readers not to sentimental enjoyment but to a radical recognition: that nature is the very mirror of spirit, that by entering the woods with an open heart one may glimpse eternity. The opening pages of his essay *Nature* remain among the most powerful passages in American literature, not for their argument alone but for the sense of dawn they convey — as if one were standing with him on the threshold of a new spiritual epoch.

Equally powerful was his call for **Self-Reliance**, which has often been misunderstood as mere individualism or rugged independence. Emerson's self-reliance was not the ego's prideful assertion, but the soul's trust in its own alignment with the divine. To rely on oneself was, for him, to listen to the whisper of intuition, to dare to trust the inner voice that speaks more truly than conformity to society's expectations. In that voice one could hear the echo of the Oversoul itself, the great Unity in which all souls participate.

The **Oversoul** was Emerson's most mystical vision: the recognition that each person carries within themselves a spark of the infinite, and that in communion with others we discover not separateness but profound unity. This was no mere philosophical proposition for him; it was a lived intuition, something that shimmered through his journals, his friendships, his sermons, and his silences. Emerson stood in Concord's quiet landscapes and felt the whole cosmos reflected there.

And yet, Emerson was no recluse. His thought was lived out in the tumult of public life. He lectured tirelessly, traveling from town to town across New England and beyond, his words stirring audiences not only with their ideas but with their cadence, their music, their daring. He spoke against slavery with increasing urgency, gave his voice to the cause of freedom, and encouraged younger writers such as Thoreau, Whitman, and Fuller to trust their own genius. He embodied the role of a mentor, not by imposing doctrines but by awakening others to their own powers.

As his life drew toward its close, memory began to falter, words slipped away, but the luminous presence remained. Visitors to his Concord home in his later years often remarked on the serenity of the man, his gentle attentiveness, as though the philosophy he had lived had finally settled into a deep stillness. He died in 1882, leaving behind not only a body of writings but a spirit that continues to breathe through American thought and beyond.

Why does Emerson matter today? Because the questions he asked are still ours. How shall we live in harmony with the natural world? How can we trust our inner voice amidst the noise of society? How can we affirm unity in a fractured age? Emerson does not give us ready-made answers. Instead, he offers us a stance, a way of seeing, a call to awaken to the divinity of our own experience. He invites us, again and again, to stand in the woods until we forget ourselves and become "a transparent eyeball," seeing not as separate beings but as expressions of the whole.

This book does not aim to systematize Emerson or reduce him to slogans. Rather, it seeks to enter into his life and words, to walk beside him through the forests of Concord, to sit with him in the lecture halls of Boston, to grieve with him at the graves of those he loved, to listen with him to the rustle of the Oversoul. It is an attempt to let his wisdom breathe anew, to allow his insights to illuminate not only the nineteenth century but the twenty-first.

We will follow his journey from childhood to maturity, from ministry to philosophy, from solitude to fellowship, from America to Europe and back again. Along the way, we will encounter the ideas that became the backbone of Transcendentalism, the friendships that sustained him, the losses that shaped him, and the legacies that endure. And we will seek, above all, to understand what it means, in our own age, to live in the spirit of Emerson's great triad: **Nature, Self-Reliance, and the Oversoul.**

To read Emerson is to be reminded that philosophy is not a matter of abstract propositions but of life itself — the living current of being that runs through trees, stars, and human hearts. He stands before us not as a distant monument, but as a companion whose words still strike with the freshness of morning air. His wisdom is not a relic but a wellspring, and to drink from it is to feel again the possibility of awakening.

Thus we begin, not with a closed doctrine, but with an open invitation: to walk with Ralph

Waldo Emerson into the woods of thought, to listen to the whisper of the leaves, and to discover, perhaps, that the voice we hear speaking is also our own.

## Childhood in Boston: Books, Loss, and the Seeds of Solitude

The child who would one day speak of the Oversoul and the majesty of self-reliance first opened his eyes in a parsonage on Summer Street in Boston, May 25, 1803. His name was Ralph Waldo Emerson, the fourth of eight children, a boy born into the austere yet vibrant atmosphere of New England's clerical families. His father, the Reverend William Emerson, was a minister of the First Church of Boston, a figure of imposing presence and stern intellect, and his mother, Ruth Haskins Emerson, carried the quiet strength that would sustain her family through storms of grief and scarcity. The Emerson household was one of books and sermons, of prayer and discipline, of the steady rhythm of religious observance woven into daily life.

From the beginning, Ralph's world was marked by fragility. He was not yet eight years old when his father died of stomach cancer, leaving the family with little money and heavy burdens. Poverty pressed upon them, and his mother and the widowed aunt Mary Moody Emerson became the twin forces that held the children together. Aunt Mary was a woman of unusual intensity — learned, pious, fiercely independent. She filled the young boy's mind with scripture, with history, with moral exhortations, impressing upon him both the sternness of duty and the boundless heights of spiritual aspiration. Ralph would later say that she taught him to "seek the highest." Her influence was like a flint striking sparks in the child's imagination.

Books became his refuge and his horizon. In the cramped rooms of the Emerson home, volumes of Milton, Plutarch, Shakespeare, and the Bible were his constant companions. He read not as a student cramming for recitation, but as one searching for voices across time that could answer the questions rising unbidden in his own heart. The cadences of Milton's blank verse and the soaring rhetoric of scripture imprinted themselves deeply in his ear, so that later, when he wrote or spoke, there was always something of that resonance, that music of the sacred, echoing through his words.

Yet this was not an idyllic childhood. Emerson knew hunger, knew the shame of patched clothes, knew the silences that follow loss. The death of his father cast a shadow across the family, and more deaths would follow. His beloved brother Charles would die young, leaving Ralph to grieve again. These early bereavements gave him a familiarity with impermanence, a sense that life is always tinged with loss. It may be that his later philosophy, so full of emphasis on the eternal currents flowing through change, had its seed in this early confrontation with transience. He learned, before he could fully articulate it, that beneath sorrow there is a deeper ground, a stillness that loss cannot destroy.

Boston itself, with its narrow streets and harbor winds, was more than a backdrop; it was part of the boy's formation. The city was a place of sermons and schools, of merchants and sailors, of old Puritan rigor giving way to the stirrings of Unitarian liberalism. Emerson absorbed the atmosphere of moral seriousness and civic engagement, the sense that ideas mattered, that words could shape lives. Even as a child he was aware of living in a community where thought and conscience were taken seriously, where books and sermons were treated as instruments of both salvation and social order.

Ralph entered the Boston Latin School, a venerable institution founded in the seventeenth century, where the discipline of Latin grammar and classical authors shaped his early education. The rigor of the school was severe, and the young boy's fragile health often faltered under the strain. Yet there was also in him a quickness of mind, an ability to seize upon ideas and turn them inward, reflecting and transforming them. He was not the brightest star among his peers, not the most dazzling in recitation, but there was already in him that depth of interiority, that habit of reflection, which set him apart.

The figure of Aunt Mary loomed large over these years. She was eccentric, sometimes difficult, yet to Ralph she represented the possibility of a life devoted entirely to the realm of spirit. She filled her letters with exhortations, with fierce calls to purity, with visions of divine grandeur. To him she was both mentor and model, embodying the conviction that life must be lived under the gaze of eternity. In her presence, the boy learned to look beyond the surface of things, to seek the invisible currents beneath appearances.

In those early years one also finds the first stirrings of solitude. Emerson was not gregarious, not drawn to crowds of children. He was shy, inward, often walking alone, thinking his own thoughts. Solitude did not weigh on him as loneliness but served as the matrix in which his imagination could germinate. He walked through Boston's streets, wandered along the edges of the harbor, sat with his books, and felt that peculiar joy of being alone and yet accompanied by invisible presences — by voices from books, by the murmur of nature, by intimations of something vast.

If childhood is the seedbed of philosophy, then Emerson's early soil was rich with paradox: poverty and abundance, loss and presence, stern discipline and imaginative freedom. He was marked by the Puritan insistence on moral seriousness, yet also given glimpses of a more expansive vision through books and reverie. The tension between constraint and liberation, between form and freedom, would become one of the leitmotifs of his mature thought.

By the time he entered Harvard College at the age of fourteen, Emerson had already carried within him the imprint of these early years: the grief that taught him impermanence, the books that taught him the music of language, the solitude that taught him to trust the inner voice. His childhood was not one of unbroken happiness, but it was one of deep formation. It gave him the vocabulary of loss, the hunger for wisdom, and the habit of seeking the eternal in the everyday.

Looking back across his life, one senses that Emerson never outgrew that boyhood sense of standing in two worlds at once: the fragile, transient world of loss and change, and the hidden, eternal world glimpsed in moments of solitude and reading. It is this doubleness that gives his later writings their peculiar depth. When he speaks of the Oversoul, it is not an abstract concept but the fulfillment of a yearning born in childhood sorrow. When he calls for self-reliance, it is not the boast of one untouched by loss, but the counsel of one who learned early that external supports may vanish and that the soul must lean upon itself.

The seeds were sown in Boston: the stern house of prayer, the stack of books on a small desk, the figure of a widowed mother and an intense aunt shaping the imagination of a boy who would one day give voice to America's spiritual independence. In those seeds lay the promise of a man who would turn grief into vision, solitude into wisdom, and the quiet of childhood into a voice that still echoes across centuries.

## Harvard Years: The Making of a Scholar and a Minister

At the age of fourteen, Ralph Waldo Emerson entered Harvard College, a boy of slight build with clear eyes and an inner life already charged with reflections beyond his years. The institution, founded in 1636 to train Puritan ministers, carried with it the weight of tradition and a reputation for rigorous scholarship. For Emerson, whose family's financial resources were strained, Harvard was both a gateway to opportunity and a crucible in which his mind and character would be tested.

He arrived not as a prodigy crowned with promise, but as a young man marked by modest confidence and a quiet intensity. Harvard in the early nineteenth century was less a university in the modern sense and more a training ground for the elite of New England society. Its curriculum was still steeped in classical studies — Latin, Greek, logic, rhetoric, moral philosophy. Mathematics and the sciences played a role, but the crown of learning was literature, theology, and the shaping of a cultivated mind. Students were ranked publicly, their standing made known by the order in which their names were called at roll or in ceremonies. Emerson, never a dazzling scholar, ranked about the middle of his class. Yet already there was in him a gift not always visible in grades: the capacity to absorb, to reflect, and to allow learning to ferment into something original.

Life at Harvard was not easy for him. Money was scarce. He waited tables for wealthier classmates, worked as a messenger, and even served as a "President's freshman," a role that meant running errands for the college president in exchange for reduced tuition. These duties humbled him, but they also ingrained a quiet independence. Emerson's poverty sharpened his sense of self-reliance, a theme that would one day become his clarion call. He knew what it was to live without abundance, to stitch together dignity from meager resources, to cultivate inward wealth when outward possessions were few.

Amidst this struggle, he turned again to books as companions and guides. The classics deepened his sense of form and eloquence. He read Homer, Plato, Cicero, Milton, Shakespeare — absorbing their cadences and their visions of human greatness. At the same time, his notebooks began to show the emergence of a personal voice, tentative but searching, eager to move beyond imitation. He wrote fragments of reflection, sketches of thought, moral observations, trying out the language that would one day carry his philosophy. Even now, in the dormitory rooms and libraries of Harvard, Emerson was rehearsing the tones of the sage he would become.

Religion still framed much of his horizon. Harvard was in transition from the stern Calvinism of its past toward the more liberal Unitarianism that would shape New England in Emerson's day. The Unitarians emphasized reason, moral character, and a benevolent God, rejecting the harsher doctrines of predestination and damnation. This liberal Christianity appealed to Emerson, offering a vision of faith compatible with conscience and rational inquiry. He prepared himself, as his lineage seemed to demand, for the ministry.

Yet doubt was already stirring. Emerson found himself drawn to the beauty of words, the force of imagination, and the immediacy of personal experience more than to the structures of dogma. He admired the pulpit as a place where one could shape hearts with language, but he was less certain about the inherited doctrines he was expected to defend. The seeds of his eventual departure from formal ministry were already sown, even as he dutifully walked the path toward ordination.

The Harvard years were not solely about study. There was the camaraderie of fellow students, long walks under elms, debates in dormitory rooms, youthful confidences whispered in corridors. Emerson was reserved, sometimes shy, but capable of deep friendship. He learned in these years how to listen, how to speak with quiet conviction, how to weave companionship from shared books and shared silences. These friendships planted in him the conviction that the soul's greatness is not only found in solitude but also in the communion of minds.

He also developed his craft as a speaker. Harvard encouraged oratory, and Emerson took to the platform with an ease that surprised some of his classmates. His voice was not thunderous, but it carried clarity and cadence. There was already that rhythm in his speech, a kind of musicality, that made his words linger in the minds of those who heard them. Though he lacked the fiery charisma of some, his earnestness and quiet authority drew attention. It was in these early exercises in oration that the future lecturer, the man who would one day address audiences across America, first found his footing.

Graduation in 1821 marked not the end of his education but the beginning of a new phase. He was only eighteen, uncertain of his path but compelled forward by necessity and by the force of family expectation. Teaching became his immediate occupation. He took positions in schools, including one run by his older brother William, where Ralph taught Latin, Greek, and other subjects to boys not much younger than himself. Teaching was both burden and discipline. It required patience, structure, the ability to communicate ideas clearly — all of which would serve him well in later years. Yet Emerson's heart was not in the classroom of children. His soul longed for something larger, something that could give full expression to the stirrings he felt when he read and when he walked alone beneath the sky.

In these years he began the lifelong habit of keeping journals, vast notebooks in which he poured his reflections, observations, and sketches of thought. These journals were not merely private diaries but seedbeds for his public essays. They became the workshop in which Emerson's philosophy took shape, line by line, fragment by fragment, until later he could refine and release them as fully formed essays and lectures. To read those early journals is to witness a mind in formation, oscillating between youthful enthusiasm and sober reflection, between inherited doctrines and nascent intuitions of a wider truth.

His studies at Harvard Divinity School, which he entered a few years later, further refined his path toward ministry. There he was trained in the art of preaching, in theology and scriptural interpretation, in the moral responsibilities of the pastor. Yet again, even as he absorbed the lessons, a subtle unease grew in him. He could not fully reconcile the grandeur of spirit he felt in nature and solitude with the constrained forms of church liturgy. His vision was expanding beyond the pulpit, though he did not yet know where it would lead.

These Harvard years, then, were a crucible: years of poverty and discipline, of immersion in the classics, of tentative steps into oratory, of friendships and doubts. Emerson left the college with no clear doctrine but with a sharpened sense of his own vocation: to live by thought, to dwell in the realm of spirit, to seek a language adequate to the truths he felt pressing within him.

Looking back, one can see how essential this period was to the making of Emerson. Without the poverty, he might never have learned the resilience and independence that later fueled his self-reliance. Without the classics, he might never have absorbed the music of language that made his prose so enduring. Without the Divinity School, he might never have confronted so directly the limits of inherited religion, and thus might never have broken free into his own path. Harvard was not the place where Emerson's philosophy was born, but it was the furnace in which his mind was tempered, the place where he acquired the tools he would later use to carve out a new spiritual vision for his age.

In his journals, written not long after leaving Harvard, he remarked that "the scholar is he of all men whom the spectacle of the present most engages." That sense of being engaged by the world, of allowing thought to rise in response to life rather than abstract systems, was already present in the young Emerson. Harvard gave him the means, but his own spirit supplied the end. He left not as a finished scholar, but as a seeker — a seeker whose path would soon lead him into the pulpit, into marriage, into loss, and finally into the freedom of his own voice.

Thus the boy of Boston, shaped by poverty and solitude, passed through the gates of Harvard and emerged as a young man with the beginnings of a vocation. He was not yet the Sage of Concord, not yet the voice of Transcendentalism, but the foundations were laid. The seeds of independence, reverence for nature, trust in intuition, and devotion to language were already germinating. The scholar had been formed, the minister was in preparation, and beyond them both, the philosopher-poet was waiting to be born.

## Ministry and Doubt: From the Pulpit to the Threshold of Freedom

When Ralph Waldo Emerson stood in the pulpit for the first time as an ordained minister, he seemed to have fulfilled both family inheritance and cultural expectation. He had passed through Harvard College and the Divinity School; he had been schooled in the rhythms of sermon and scripture, in the art of consolation and moral exhortation. He was, outwardly, exactly what his lineage prepared him to be: another in a long line of Emerson preachers, carrying forward the clerical mantle of New England. And yet, beneath the surface of that steady vocation, something restless moved within him — a current of doubt, of questioning, of hunger for a truth more immediate than any creed could contain.

The ministry of Emerson began at Boston's Second Church, where he was called to serve in 1829. He was twenty-six, earnest, thoughtful, already marked by the quiet dignity that would characterize him throughout life. His sermons were elegant and measured, filled with moral insight and literary allusion. Parishioners admired his seriousness, his ability to weave together scripture and reflection, his tone of calm authority. To many he seemed an ideal pastor. Yet

Emerson himself was uneasy. He delivered the words, but behind them he felt an absence. Something in him longed not merely to interpret doctrine but to speak from the immediacy of experience.

The young minister was also a young husband. In 1829 he married Ellen Louisa Tucker, a bright and delicate woman whose presence brought joy into his otherwise serious life. She was radiant, affectionate, deeply cherished by Emerson. Their marriage, however, was shadowed almost immediately by illness. Ellen suffered from tuberculosis, and within less than two years she was gone. Emerson, at twenty-seven, found himself standing at her grave, bereft and shaken. The grief hollowed him, pressed him into silence, forced him into questions that the pulpit could not answer. The death of his father in childhood had wounded him; the death of his wife opened a fissure in his soul that would never entirely close.

It was in the aftermath of Ellen's passing that Emerson's doubt deepened into crisis. The rituals of the church, particularly the administration of the Lord's Supper, came to feel hollow to him. He could not reconcile the living presence of spirit he intuited in nature and in his own heart with the formality of bread and wine passed in solemn ritual. To him, the rite had lost its vitality, had become an empty form. He found himself increasingly unable to stand in the pulpit and administer what he did not inwardly affirm.

His sermons during this period reveal the tension. On the one hand, they are filled with calls to moral earnestness, with eloquent expositions of scripture. On the other, they contain hints of his later philosophy: references to the inner light, to the immediacy of God's presence, to the call to trust one's own intuition. The voice of the minister and the voice of the transcendentalist were already mingling, though not yet fully distinct.

Finally, in 1832, Emerson resigned his pulpit. In his farewell sermon he explained, with candor and calm, that he could no longer in good conscience administer the Lord's Supper. He did not condemn the rite, nor did he attack the church, but he declared that for him, truth must be sought in freer ways. His congregation was shocked. Some were pained, others indignant, but Emerson remained serene. He was stepping into uncertainty, relinquishing the security of position and income, but he could not do otherwise. His conscience demanded freedom.

This resignation marked a turning point, not only in Emerson's life but in American thought. For here was a man willing to follow his inner conviction even at the cost of career and tradition. His act was not rebellion for its own sake; it was fidelity to the whisper of spirit within. The same fidelity would later form the core of his essay *Self-Reliance*. In leaving the pulpit, Emerson paradoxically became more of a minister than ever: a minister not bound to one church, but to the wider congregation of humanity, called to awaken souls through word and example.

In the months following his resignation, Emerson traveled. He journeyed to Europe, carrying with him his grief, his journals, and his longing for a new horizon. In Paris he wandered the Jardin des Plantes, marveling at the profusion of life, the diversity of forms, the sheer abundance of nature. In England he met Coleridge, Wordsworth, and above all Thomas Carlyle, with whom he formed a friendship that would last a lifetime. These encounters nourished him, but they also confirmed his independence. He admired their genius, but he knew his own voice must not be derivative. He was an American, and his task was to articulate the wisdom of his own soil.

Looking back, one sees that the crisis of ministry was essential to the birth of Emerson's philosophy. Without the weight of expectation, he might never have discovered the freedom of thought that defined him. Without the grief of Ellen's death, he might never have plumbed the depths of sorrow that gave his later serenity its foundation. Without the courage to resign, he might never have embodied the very self-reliance he would later proclaim.

What Emerson discovered in those years was that doubt, far from being an enemy of faith, can be its most faithful companion. Doubt, for him, was the refusal to settle for secondhand belief, the insistence on testing inherited forms against the immediacy of experience. His doubt was not skepticism in the shallow sense but reverence for truth in its most living form. It was doubt that led him beyond the pulpit and into the woods, beyond the chalice of communion and into the vast sacrament of nature.

Thus the minister became the philosopher, the parish priest became the sage of Concord. By following his doubt, Emerson crossed a threshold into freedom, and in that freedom he found a voice that continues to awaken. The boy shaped by Boston's poverty, the student tempered at Harvard, the minister tested by grief — all converged in this moment of departure. From here, the path of Emerson's life would widen into the great arc of essays, lectures, friendships, and visions that made him the voice of a new America.

## Journeys to Europe: Wordsworth, Coleridge, and Conversations with Carlyle

When Ralph Waldo Emerson set sail for Europe in 1832, he carried with him the weight of grief and the lightness of newfound freedom. He had resigned from the pulpit of Boston's Second Church, relinquished the prescribed duties of the ministry, and stepped into a future uncharted. The death of Ellen had torn open a void in his life, but into that void streamed a yearning to see, to learn, to encounter the great minds whose words had shaped him from afar. He boarded ship not only as a traveler but as a seeker, carrying with him a journal, a modest purse, and the quiet determination to find his own path.

The voyage itself was arduous, as all Atlantic crossings were in that era. The ship heaved and groaned under the weight of storms; passengers were confined for days to narrow quarters; the sea stretched endlessly in all directions. Emerson, prone to seasickness, spent much of the journey in discomfort, yet he also used the long hours to reflect, to write, to imagine the horizons that awaited him. Already in his journals one finds lines in which he transfigures the rolling ocean into a symbol of the infinite, into a mirror of the

Oversoul whose currents he felt moving through all things.

He arrived first in Italy, where the ruins of Rome and the art of Florence spoke to him in ways both inspiring and alien. The grandeur of antiquity impressed him, but he remained conscious of being an American, the child of a young nation. He admired the beauty of European culture, yet he did not feel called to dwell within it. For Emerson, Italy was a gallery of marvels, but not his spiritual home. He longed for living voices, not only silent stones.

It was in England that he found those voices. He made his way to the Lake District, the home of William Wordsworth. Wordsworth was already a legendary figure, the poet of nature whose lines had awakened in readers across the world a reverence for the ordinary, a recognition of the sacred in the commonplace. Emerson approached him with the reverence of a disciple approaching a master. Their meeting, however, was tinged with disappointment. Wordsworth, in his later years, had grown conservative, cautious, attached to institutions and wary of radical enthusiasm. Emerson respected the poet but found his spirit diminished, his youthful fire cooled into convention. Still, the encounter mattered: it reminded Emerson that genius, once vital, can ossify if it clings too tightly to form.

From Wordsworth he traveled to see Samuel Taylor Coleridge, the philosopher-poet whose writings on imagination and theology had long stirred him. Coleridge was brilliant but diffuse, a torrent of ideas spilling out in conversation, many unfinished, many contradictory. Emerson listened with fascination, but also with discernment. He saw in Coleridge a mind of immense power, yet one unable to distill its insights into clarity. Emerson would later remark that Coleridge "talks eternally, and is never once understood." The encounter was instructive. From Coleridge he learned not only about imagination but also about the dangers of excessive abstraction, the need to ground thought in lived clarity.

The most important encounter of all came in Scotland, with Thomas Carlyle. Carlyle, then living in rural Craigenputtock with his wife Jane, was at the beginning of his own fame as a historian and essayist. Emerson traveled across the moors to meet him, and in Carlyle he found a kindred spirit. Their temperaments were different — Carlyle fierce, stormy, given to fiery denunciations; Emerson calm, measured, seeking harmony. Yet beneath these differences lay a shared conviction: that the modern world needed voices of truth, men who could speak from conscience rather than convention.

The meeting between Carlyle and Emerson has become one of the legendary encounters of literary history. They walked the Scottish fields, talked by the fireside, shared their visions of society and spirit. Carlyle recognized in Emerson a younger ally across the Atlantic, someone who could carry forth a gospel of moral seriousness in a new land. Emerson, in turn, found in Carlyle both inspiration and warning: inspiration in his passion, warning in his bitterness. The two men formed a friendship that would last a lifetime, sustained by an extraordinary correspondence that bridged the ocean. Through their letters, Carlyle thundered forth his critiques of industrial civilization, while Emerson replied with serene reflections on spirit and freedom. Together they formed a dialogue that enriched both, even as each remained rooted in his own soil.

Travel, for Emerson, was never mere sightseeing. He was not drawn to the grandeur of cathedrals or the pomp of courts. He sought, rather, what he called "living books" — men and women whose lives embodied ideas. In Europe he saw both the glory and the decay of civilization: the weight of tradition, the brilliance of art, but also the ossification of thought into institutions. For him, Europe was a mirror in which he saw more clearly the task awaiting America: to create a culture not derivative of the Old World, but fresh, vital, rooted in its own nature.

The journey also deepened his sense of solitude. He traveled much of the time alone, walking through cities and countryside, observing, reflecting, writing in his journal. He noted how travel strips away the familiar, leaving the soul exposed to its own resources. "Travel," he later wrote, "is a fool's paradise," meaning that one cannot escape oneself by changing place. And yet, paradoxically, by journeying far he discovered more fully his own independence. The foreign sharpened his sense of home; the grandeur of Europe clarified his allegiance to the young America.

In Paris, he visited the Jardin des Plantes, a vast botanical and zoological garden, where he marveled at the diversity of forms of life. The array of species, meticulously arranged, struck him with the force of revelation. Here was nature's abundance, its creativity, its ceaseless innovation. He saw in the natural world not chaos but a hidden order, a law of form manifesting through infinite variety. This experience would echo through his later essay *Nature,* where he speaks of the "Universal Being" manifest in every leaf and stone.

By the time Emerson returned to America in 1833, he was no longer a minister without a pulpit but a thinker with a mission. The encounters with Wordsworth, Coleridge, and Carlyle had shown him both the heights and the limits of European genius. The ruins of Rome and the cathedrals of Paris had reminded him of the grandeur of history but also of its weight. Above all, his own solitude, sharpened by grief and widened by travel, had crystallized his conviction that the divine speaks most directly through the soul itself and through the living book of nature.

Thus the journey to Europe, undertaken in the aftermath of loss, became the threshold of Emerson's mature voice. He returned not with doctrines borrowed from others but with the courage to trust his own insight. He had seen the Old World, admired it, and let it go. He was ready now to speak as an American, to declare that revelation was not confined to the past or to distant lands, but present in every tree of Concord, in every intuition of the human heart.

Travel had given him not answers but confirmation: confirmation that the true task was not imitation but creation, not the repetition of

Europe's wisdom but the birth of a new wisdom suited to America. Emerson came home prepared to write the words that would ignite Transcendentalism, to lecture with the authority of one who had seen and weighed the Old World, and to live with the serenity of one who trusted the Oversoul more than any institution.

The minister had become the philosopher. The seeker had become the sage in preparation. Europe had given him voices, but America would give him his own.

## Breaking Away: The Divinity School Address and the Spark of Revolution

On a warm evening in July 1838, in the quiet town of Cambridge, Ralph Waldo Emerson stood before the graduating class of Harvard Divinity School. The setting was intimate: a modest chapel, a gathering of young men preparing to step into the pulpits of New England, professors and clergy seated in expectation. Emerson himself, thirty-five years old, slender, composed, with that gentle authority that marked him, had been invited to deliver an address. What transpired that night would be remembered as a watershed moment in American religious thought, the spark that lit the fires of Transcendentalism in its most public form.

The speech he gave — now known simply as the *Divinity School Address* — was not a formal theological treatise but a living manifesto. Emerson spoke not as a scholar defending doctrine but as a man testifying to experience. He told the young ministers that true religion is not inherited ritual, not the repetition of secondhand truths, not the frozen dogmas of tradition. True religion, he insisted, is the immediate experience of the divine within the soul, the living presence of God felt directly in the heart and in nature.

"The soul," he declared, "knows no persons. It invites every man to expand to the full circle of the universe, and will have no preferences but those of spontaneous love." These words carried both beauty and danger. They affirmed that the divine is not mediated through priest or sacrament, but encountered directly in the self. He spoke of Jesus not as a distant figure to be worshipped, but as one who realized his unity with God and showed others the path to the same realization. Christ was an exemplar, not an exception. In making this claim, Emerson undermined the authority of the church as mediator and placed the weight of revelation squarely upon the individual soul.

To the young graduates, his words were electrifying. They were being told that their true task was not to preserve forms but to awaken life, not to echo creeds but to stir the sleeping divinity within each person. Emerson's vision called them to become not defenders of tradition but heralds of a new dawn, where every man and woman could stand in the light of their own intuition.

But to the established clergy who listened, and to the Harvard faculty who soon heard reports of the address, his words were shocking, even heretical. To speak of the insufficiency of miracles, to call the church stale, to claim that revelation is continuous and personal — these were radical assertions in a culture still deeply tied to inherited forms of Christianity. The backlash was swift. Ministers denounced him, newspapers criticized him, Harvard itself closed its doors to him for thirty years. Emerson had broken decisively with institutional religion.

Yet he did not speak as a rebel seeking to destroy, but as a lover of spirit seeking to liberate. His tone was calm, serene, almost tender. He did not rage against the church; he simply declared that life is greater than any institution, that God cannot be confined to a wafer or a book, that the soul's immediate experience is the true sanctuary. He embodied in that moment the very self-reliance he urged upon others: the courage to stand alone, to trust one's own vision even against the weight of tradition.

The *Divinity School Address* must be seen in the broader context of America in the 1830s. It was a time of religious ferment, with revivalist movements sweeping across the land, Methodists and Baptists drawing crowds with fervent preaching, while Unitarians sought a more rational and benevolent faith. Emerson's voice cut through both enthusiasm and rationalism with something deeper: the insistence that truth is not merely to be believed or argued, but to be lived.

He stood at the intersection of tradition and modernity, pointing beyond both toward a religion of the heart.

The consequences of that evening were profound. Emerson's public reputation shifted. To some he became a prophet, to others a dangerous radical. But for himself, the address was simply an act of fidelity. He had spoken what he knew to be true, and the world must take it as it would. In the months and years that followed, he turned increasingly to lectures and essays as his mode of ministry, addressing not one parish but the larger public, not a congregation of the faithful but the seekers of a nation.

What gave the *Divinity School Address* its enduring power was not merely its critique but its vision. Emerson spoke of the universe as a living whole, of the soul as a spark of the divine, of morality as the natural flowering of a spirit attuned to truth. He urged the young ministers to preach "the sentiment of virtue, that it is a part of man, and that it is universal." He called them to trust intuition, to listen for the inner voice that speaks with greater authority than any tradition.

In these words we hear the early notes of what would become his great themes: nature as revelation, self-reliance as fidelity to the inner voice, the Oversoul as the unity of all being. The address was not an isolated moment but the threshold into Emerson's mature philosophy. It was the public declaration of what had been forming in solitude, now spoken aloud with clarity and courage.

And yet, the address also reveals the cost of fidelity. Emerson was cut off from Harvard, criticized by peers, cast as an outsider in the very community that had nurtured him. He bore this with serenity, but it marked him. From this point onward, he knew he must walk his own path, often apart from institutions. The loneliness of the prophet became his share. But he did not resist it; he embraced it as the price of truth.

The *Divinity School Address* remains one of the seminal texts in American thought. It crystallized the spirit of Transcendentalism, declaring that the soul is sovereign, that nature is sacred, that revelation is continuous. It signaled a break not only with Harvard but with the very notion that truth is mediated by external authority. In that small chapel in 1838, Emerson declared a revolution — not political but spiritual, not loud but quiet, a revolution of the inward eye.

When he walked away from Harvard that evening, he had no way of knowing how enduring his words would be. He could only sense that he had spoken from necessity, from the pressure of spirit within. The young ministers who heard him carried those words into their own lives, some with enthusiasm, others with caution, but none untouched. A seed had been planted, a spark kindled, that would continue to burn long after the echoes of that summer evening faded.

For Emerson himself, the address was not an end but a beginning. It marked the moment when he ceased to be a minister of a church and became a minister of the Oversoul. From here his essays would flow — *Nature, Self-Reliance, The Over-Soul* — each an elaboration of the vision declared that night. He had broken away, and in breaking away he had found his voice.

## The Call of Nature: Forests, Rivers, and the American Scripture

When Ralph Waldo Emerson published *Nature* in 1836, he was thirty-three years old, already known as a lecturer, recently remarried, and living in Concord. It was a slender volume, fewer than a hundred pages, privately printed and modest in circulation. Yet its appearance marked one of the decisive moments in American thought, for in its pages Emerson declared that the fields, rivers, and skies of the New World were themselves a scripture, a book of revelation written not on vellum but upon leaves and clouds.

The writing of *Nature* was not an abstract exercise. It was born of long walks in the forests around Concord, of hours spent by the riverbanks, of solitary reverie under the stars. Emerson had always carried within him the sense that nature was more than backdrop; it was presence, language, spirit. In *Nature* he gave voice to that sense, and in doing so he redefined the relation between human beings and the world they inhabit.

"Standing on the bare ground," he wrote, "my head bathed by the blithe air, and uplifted into infinite space, all mean egotism vanishes. I become a transparent eyeball; I am nothing; I see all; the currents of the Universal Being circulate through me; I am part or particle of God." Few sentences in American literature are as famous, or as strange. In them we hear the fusion of mystical vision and New World immediacy. The "transparent eyeball" is not a philosophical concept but an image of pure perception, where the self dissolves into openness and sees the world not as separate objects but as living revelation.

To enter nature, for Emerson, was to enter a temple. Not a temple built of stone but one without walls, where the columns were trees and the hymns were sung by the wind. The divine was not confined to church liturgy but revealed itself in the rustle of leaves, the shimmer of light on water, the flight of birds at dusk. He was not romanticizing nature as pastoral charm; he was recognizing it as the very garment of spirit. To walk into the woods was to read scripture written by the hand of God.

This vision was profoundly American. In Europe, Emerson had admired the ruins of Rome and the cathedrals of Paris, but he returned convinced that the true revelation for his people lay not in inherited monuments but in the vast landscapes of their own land. The American continent, with its forests stretching beyond horizon, its rivers flowing untamed, its skies of unbounded clarity, was itself a book of wisdom awaiting readers. Emerson's *Nature* was the first attempt to teach his countrymen how to read that book.

The philosophy articulated there was radical. He declared that nature is not a collection of objects for human use but a living whole in which the human spirit participates. He urged his readers to look beyond utilitarian purposes — beyond timber, beyond crops, beyond profit — and to recognize nature as symbol, as teacher, as mirror of the soul. "The world is emblematic," he wrote; every natural fact is a symbol of a spiritual fact. The flowing river speaks of time, the seasons of renewal, the tree of rootedness and growth. To live attentively in nature is to dwell already in revelation.

For Emerson, this was not pantheism in the crude sense of equating God with material things. It was a recognition that spirit and matter are not two but one, that the divine flows through the forms of the world, that to touch a leaf with reverence is to brush against eternity. He did not deny transcendence; he insisted that transcendence is immanent, that the eternal is present here and now, in the shining of dew, in the flight of geese across an autumn sky.

The essay also called for a new kind of scholar, a new kind of poet. The "American Scholar," whom Emerson would soon describe in a famous lecture, was to be one who read not only books but the book of nature, who learned not merely from tradition but from the living present. Nature was to be the primary text, and the scholar was to be its interpreter. Emerson envisioned an intellectual life not derivative from Europe but grounded in the soil of America, attuned to its seasons, its landscapes, its possibilities.

The reception of *Nature* was modest at first. Only a small circle of readers grasped its significance. But within that circle — including Thoreau, Margaret Fuller, and Bronson Alcott — the book ignited a sense of mission. It gave articulation to what many had felt: that the land itself was calling for a new voice, a new vision, a new way of dwelling in the world. It became, in retrospect, the foundational text of Transcendentalism.

The force of the book lay not in argument but in invitation. Emerson did not seek to prove propositions; he sought to awaken perception. He invited his readers to go outside, to look at the stars until they felt awe, to walk in the woods until they forgot themselves, to see that nature is not mute matter but living presence. His style itself carried the cadence of revelation —

aphoristic, luminous, suggestive, like shafts of light breaking through forest branches.

Yet behind this vision lay Emerson's own struggle. He had known grief, poverty, doubt. He had resigned from the church, turned away from inherited certainties. What remained for him was the immediacy of experience, the sense that life itself is divine. *Nature* was not the work of a naïve optimist but of one who had passed through shadow and found light not in distant heaven but in the very ground underfoot. The forests and rivers of Concord became his scripture because they spoke to him with a freshness no ritual could equal.

Walking through those landscapes, Emerson discovered that solitude is not emptiness but plenitude. To be alone in the woods was to be accompanied by the whole. He felt the Oversoul whispering through branches, circulating through air and water, reminding him that separateness is illusion. This discovery gave him serenity: even in grief, even in loss, one is never truly alone, for one participates in the vast life of the universe.

Thus, the call of nature in Emerson's life was not an aesthetic preference but a spiritual vocation. He heard in the wind a summons, in the river a teaching, in the forest a scripture. He answered that call by writing *Nature,* and in doing so, he gave to America its first great philosophical declaration rooted in its own soil. He showed his contemporaries that revelation is not confined to the past but is ongoing, that the divine speaks now, here, in the rustle of grass, in the gaze of stars, in the transparent silence of being.

## Self-Reliance: The Courage to Trust the Inner Light

If *Nature* was Emerson's scripture of the outer world, then *Self-Reliance* was his gospel of the inner. Published in 1841 as part of his first series of essays, it quickly became his most celebrated and controversial work, the piece most quoted, most debated, most misinterpreted. For in those pages Emerson placed before his readers a challenge as bracing as a New England winter wind: trust thyself.

The essay begins with a simple assertion: "To believe your own thought, to believe that what is true for you in your private heart is true for all men — that is genius." With these words Emerson set fire to complacency. He was telling his contemporaries that authority does not lie in tradition, nor in institutions, nor in the opinions of others, but in the spark of intuition within the individual soul. To live authentically is to listen to that inner voice and to act upon it, even when it contradicts society, even when it isolates you.

The call to self-reliance was not new in human history. One can find it in the Stoics of Greece and Rome, in the mystics of every age. But Emerson spoke it with a distinctly American accent, in a young nation that valued independence but often shrank from intellectual daring. He told his readers that conformity is the death of vitality, that consistency for its own sake is the hobgoblin of little minds, that greatness lies in being misunderstood. These aphorisms, scattered like sparks through the essay, have since been repeated endlessly, sometimes stripped of their depth, sometimes turned into slogans of rugged individualism. Yet at their heart they express something more subtle: the courage to trust the inner light.

Emerson was not calling for selfishness or arrogance. He did not mean that one should assert ego against others. What he meant was fidelity to the Oversoul's whisper in one's own heart. Each person, he believed, carries within themselves a ray of the universal, an intuition of truth that, if trusted, will align them with the whole. To betray that inner voice by conformity is to betray one's own divinity. To trust it is to participate in the living truth that circulates through all.

He illustrated this with images drawn from daily life. Children, he noted, embody self-reliance naturally. They speak their minds without fear, act without excessive regard for appearances, live in the immediacy of their own being. Society, by contrast, trains us to mask ourselves, to seek approval, to conform to expectations. The task of the adult, Emerson declared, is to recover that original integrity, to live once more from the center rather than from the circumference.

This teaching was not abstract for him; it was lived. When he resigned from the ministry, when he delivered the *Divinity School Address,* when he wrote *Nature,* he was practicing self-reliance. He knew the cost of standing alone, the loneliness of being misunderstood, the sting of criticism. Yet he also knew the serenity that comes from fidelity to conscience. His essay was not the exhortation of a comfortable man but the testimony of one who had risked reputation and livelihood for the sake of truth.

The style of *Self-Reliance* mirrors its message. It is not a systematic argument but a series of luminous declarations, each a burst of intuition, each demanding response. The essay moves like a river of fire, leaping from aphorism to image, never pausing to justify, always pressing forward with conviction. Emerson was less concerned to prove than to provoke, less to instruct than to awaken. He wanted his readers to feel the shock of recognition, to hear in his words the echo of their own buried insight.

The impact was immense. For some, the essay was liberating, a summons to authenticity, a declaration of independence for the soul. For others, it was troubling, even dangerous. Critics accused him of undermining social order, of encouraging arrogance, of dismissing tradition. Yet Emerson remained unperturbed. He knew that every great idea must pass through misunderstanding. Indeed, he welcomed it. "To be great," he wrote, "is to be misunderstood."

What, then, does it mean to live self-reliantly? For Emerson, it means to act from the present moment rather than from the past, to speak what one now believes even if it contradicts what one said yesterday. It means to refuse the chains of consistency when they no longer serve truth. It means to stand alone in one's conviction even against the crowd. It means to recognize that the same power that inspired Moses and Plato is present in you, waiting to be trusted.

This was a radical democratization of genius. Emerson told his readers that greatness is not reserved for the few, not confined to prophets or sages of the past. Every person has access to the divine, every soul can hear the inner voice. The only requirement is courage — the courage to trust it.

Yet he also knew the difficulty. Society, he warned, is a conspiracy against the manhood of every one of its members. It demands conformity, rewards compliance, punishes deviation. To resist it requires strength. That strength, Emerson insisted, does not come from obstinacy or pride but from the quiet assurance that one's intuition is aligned with the Oversoul. Self-reliance is not isolation but communion, not withdrawal into ego but participation in the universal through one's own particularity.

In Concord, where he wrote, Emerson lived this philosophy in daily rhythms. He tended his garden, walked the fields, conversed with friends, lectured to audiences. His life was simple, but it radiated integrity. He did not merely write about self-reliance; he embodied it in his choice to step outside the institutions that could have secured him comfort. He chose instead the precarious freedom of the independent lecturer and essayist, relying on the strength of his thought and the resonance of his words.

*Self-Reliance* remains, even today, a text that disturbs and awakens. It asks each reader: Do you trust your own thought? Do you dare to live from the center of your being? Or do you hide behind conformity, behind the borrowed opinions of others? The essay does not comfort; it challenges. It does not soothe; it demands. And in that demand lies its enduring power.

For Emerson, to trust the inner light was the essence of wisdom. All else — institutions, traditions, reputations — are secondary. What matters is that one be faithful to the voice of spirit within, that one dare to speak what one sees, that one live in alignment with the Oversoul. This is self-reliance: not arrogance, not isolation, but the courage to be what one is, to let the divine speak through the particularity of one's own soul.

Thus the essay, like a clear New England morning, still calls across the years. Trust thyself. Speak today what you see today. Stand alone if need be. For in that solitude you will discover not emptiness but communion, not weakness but strength, not isolation but the vast presence of the whole.

## The Oversoul: Mystical Unity and the Deep Presence of Spirit

Among all the words Emerson left us, none carry a more mystical resonance than "the Oversoul." It is the name he gave to that vast, ineffable presence which binds all beings together, the unity behind multiplicity, the eternal within the transient. For many, it remains the most enigmatic of his concepts, shimmering between philosophy and poetry, between theology and vision. Yet for Emerson it was not abstraction but experience — a reality he felt coursing through solitude, through nature, through the communion of souls.

The essay *The Over-Soul*, first published in 1841, came after years of reflection, journaling, and speaking on themes of unity. In it, Emerson attempted to give expression to what had long haunted his thought: the intuition that every soul is not isolated but part of a greater whole, that beneath the separateness of individuals there lies one shared life. "Within man," he wrote, "is the soul of the whole; the wise silence; the universal beauty, to which every part and particle is equally related; the eternal One." In these lines we hear not the voice of a logician but of a seer.

The Oversoul was Emerson's way of naming what other traditions have called God, Brahman,

Tao, or the Absolute. Yet his genius was to speak of it without dogma, to clothe it in a language free from sectarian bounds. It was at once transcendent and immanent: beyond all things and yet present in each. To feel the Oversoul was to recognize that one's own consciousness is not private property but a wave upon a vast ocean of spirit.

Where did Emerson learn this vision? Partly from books — from the Neoplatonists like Plotinus, from Eastern scriptures beginning to circulate in translation, from the mystics of Christian tradition. But more deeply, he learned it from direct experience. In his journals we find records of moments of rapture in nature, moments when self dissolved and he felt permeated by presence. Standing in a field, gazing at the stars, or walking through woods, he would suddenly know himself as more than Ralph Waldo Emerson, minister's son, lecturer, husband, father. He would feel himself as a conduit of something vast, timeless, serene. The Oversoul was his name for that reality.

The essay itself reads like scripture, not in the sense of commandments but in the sense of luminous utterances. "The soul in man," he wrote, "is not an organ, but animates and exercises all the organs; is not a function, like the power of memory, of calculation, of comparison, but uses these as hands and feet; is not a faculty, but a light; is not the intellect or the will, but the master of the intellect and the will." In passages such as these, one feels the language straining toward what cannot be fully captured, reaching for images adequate to the infinite.

The Oversoul was not only a metaphysical idea but a moral one. Emerson believed that when we recognize our participation in the Oversoul, we awaken to compassion. For if the same spirit dwells in all, then to harm another is to harm oneself, to love another is to love the whole. This conviction underlay his friendship, his politics, his mentoring of younger writers. It was not mere sentiment but ontological recognition: unity is the truth of being, and love is its natural expression.

Yet Emerson was careful not to collapse individuality into undifferentiated oneness. Each soul, he insisted, is unique, bearing its own genius, its own task. Self-reliance and the Oversoul are not contradictory but complementary. To trust oneself is to trust that the Oversoul speaks through one's particular intuition. Individuality is not erased by unity but fulfilled in it. Just as each leaf reveals the life of the tree, so each person reveals the Oversoul in their own form.

The idea resonated deeply with some of his contemporaries and baffled others. To the rationalist Unitarians, it seemed too vague, too mystical. To the orthodox, it seemed heretical, dissolving the personal God into abstraction. But to the seekers — Thoreau, Margaret Fuller, Bronson Alcott, and later Whitman — it was revelation. It gave voice to what they too had felt in moments of ecstasy and insight: that life is not fragments but a whole, that the divine is not distant but immediate.

The Oversoul also shaped Emerson's understanding of death. Having known profound loss, he sought a way to affirm continuity beyond grief. In the Oversoul he found assurance that no soul is ever lost, that each participates in the eternal, that death is not annihilation but return. When his young son Waldo died in 1842, Emerson's heart broke, but his writings reveal the comfort he found in believing that the child's soul was still within the great unity, not gone but gathered. The Oversoul was not only philosophy; it was solace.

To stand in the presence of the Oversoul is, Emerson suggested, to feel a serenity beyond circumstance, a trust that transcends fear. He described it as the "wise silence" that surrounds and permeates all. When we quiet the noise of ego, when we let go of anxious striving, we hear that silence, and in it we recognize ourselves as more than separate individuals. We discover the ground of being itself, radiant, inexhaustible.

The influence of this vision has been vast. It echoes in Thoreau's *Walden,* in Whitman's *Leaves of Grass,* in countless American voices that celebrate unity with nature and with humanity. It anticipates later currents of psychology and spirituality that speak of collective unconscious, cosmic consciousness, or universal mind. Emerson's Oversoul is the ancestor of many modern intuitions about the interconnection of all life.

For Emerson, however, it was never a theory to be debated but a truth to be lived. He urged his readers not to argue about the Oversoul but to open themselves to its presence, to trust the flashes of intuition that reveal unity, to cultivate a life of simplicity and openness where the divine can be felt. His prose was a lantern, not a cage — it illuminated but did not enclose.

In the end, the Oversoul was Emerson's way of naming the mystery at the heart of existence, a mystery that cannot be dissected but only entered. To read him is to feel the invitation to that entry: to step beyond ego, beyond separateness, into the recognition that we are all part and particle of God.

Thus the man of Concord, walking his quiet paths, gave to the world a vision as vast as the sky. In the Oversoul he saw not an idea but a reality shimmering through every leaf and every star, a presence available to every heart. To awaken to it is to live with a courage and serenity that no loss can extinguish.

## Friendship and the Communion of Souls

Of all the human bonds that shaped Emerson's life and philosophy, none carried for him the depth of meaning as friendship. Love, in its romantic form, had brought him joy and piercing grief with the early death of Ellen. Family ties, though marked by affection, were tinged with the solemn weight of New England discipline. But friendship, as he conceived and lived it, was something larger — not merely social comfort, not the exchange of companionship to ward off loneliness, but a communion of souls, a glimpse of the Oversoul refracted through another human being.

In 1841, the same year he published *Self-Reliance* and *The Over-Soul,* Emerson also published his essay *Friendship.* In its pages, one can feel his attempt to articulate the sanctity he found in human bonds that were neither familial nor romantic but spiritual. "The essence of friendship is entireness, a total magnanimity and trust," he wrote. For him, friendship was a meeting of whole beings, where nothing is hidden, where each is seen in the light of the other, where the usual defenses of social life fall away.

The essay was not theory but testimony. Emerson had lived friendship intensely, with a seriousness that sometimes bewildered his acquaintances. He gave himself wholly to those he trusted, sought them with the passion of a pilgrim, and expected in return a depth of sincerity rarely found in casual relations. To Emerson, a friend was not an ornament of life but a revelation — the soul recognizing itself in another.

From his youth onward, Emerson cultivated such bonds. With his brothers, especially Charles, he shared not only family but intellectual intimacy, writing letters of extraordinary tenderness. Charles's early death in 1836 struck Emerson deeply, and in mourning him he discovered the way friendship transfigures loss: though the person is gone, the communion remains. The Oversoul assures that no true connection is severed. In memory, in spirit, the friend endures.

Later, with Margaret Fuller, he found an interlocutor of unusual brilliance. Their friendship was not without tension — Fuller was fierce, demanding, unwilling to remain in the shadow of any man — yet Emerson cherished her as an equal in thought and as a soul who challenged him to deeper honesty. Their conversations at Concord and in Boston salons shaped the intellectual life of the Transcendentalist circle. Emerson once said that

Fuller "belonged to the soul," meaning that her presence carried the mark of the eternal.

With Henry David Thoreau, the friendship was quieter, more enigmatic. Thoreau came to live in Emerson's household for a time, tending the garden, accompanying him on walks, absorbing from him the courage to trust intuition. Emerson admired Thoreau's independence, his refusal to bow to convention, his devotion to nature. Yet their friendship was not always easy; Emerson sometimes found Thoreau prickly, and Thoreau sometimes felt overshadowed by Emerson's stature. Still, beneath these tensions ran a bond that endured: each recognized in the other a fidelity to conscience, a life lived in accord with inner truth.

What Emerson sought in friendship was not constant companionship but rare intensity. He valued solitude too deeply to desire endless company. But when he met a kindred soul, he wanted the encounter to be absolute, stripped of pretenses, luminous with sincerity. "A friend," he wrote, "is a person with whom I may be sincere. Before him, I may think aloud." That freedom — to think aloud without fear of judgment — was, for him, the heart of friendship.

Friendship also revealed to Emerson the social dimension of the Oversoul. If the Oversoul is the unity of all, then friendship is the place where that unity shines most clearly between two persons. In a friend, one feels the presence of the eternal, the assurance that behind the separateness of bodies and biographies lies one shared life. Friendship becomes sacrament: a visible sign of invisible communion.

This vision carried ethical implications. To truly honor a friend is to honor the divinity within them, to refuse to reduce them to utility, to respect their freedom, to rejoice in their uniqueness. Emerson warned against turning friendship into mere flattery or habit. He demanded of it authenticity. Better to have one true friend than many shallow acquaintances. For one true friend mirrors the whole.

In practice, Emerson's friendships were sometimes intense to the point of strain. He could overwhelm others with his expectations, or withdraw suddenly into solitude when disappointed. Yet even these difficulties reveal the seriousness with which he approached the bond. Friendship, for him, was no casual pastime; it was a spiritual vocation.

His lectures, his essays, his letters — all were imbued with this sense that life is made luminous by communion. He spoke to audiences as if to friends, desiring not to instruct but to awaken, not to dominate but to share the spark of insight. Those who heard him often remarked on the personal quality of his address, as though he were speaking directly to the innermost self of each listener. In this sense, Emerson extended the intimacy of friendship to the public sphere, treating all as potential companions in the search for truth.

The later years of his life saw many friendships ripen into serene companionship. With Carlyle, despite oceans of difference in temperament and geography, he maintained a lifelong correspondence, each letter an exchange of soul. With Bronson Alcott, eccentric and impractical though he was, Emerson found a companion in speculative thought. With women of Concord society, he cultivated bonds of respect and trust, valuing their intelligence at a time when women were often denied such recognition.

For Emerson, the test of any philosophy was whether it deepened human life. The Oversoul, self-reliance, nature — all these were not abstractions but realities to be lived. And friendship was where they converged. In the friend, one sees the Oversoul refracted. In the courage to be sincere with a friend, one practices self-reliance. In walking with a friend through fields and woods, one feels nature sanctified. Friendship became the crucible where Emerson's thought found embodiment.

Even as his memory failed in later years, even as words slipped away, visitors to his Concord home found him still radiant with the gentleness of friendship. He greeted them with warmth, with presence, as if to say that though intellect falters, the bond of souls endures. His life testified that friendship is not an ornament to philosophy but its fulfillment.

Thus, in Emerson's wisdom, friendship is more than affection. It is the communion of souls in the light of the Oversoul. It is the courage to be sincere, the joy of recognition, the sacrament of human presence. To have known even one such friend, he believed, is to have touched eternity.

## Love, Beauty, and the Transparent Eye

To understand Emerson's vision of life, one must see how deeply he wove together love and beauty with his metaphysical sense of unity. For him, love was not merely passion or personal affection, nor was beauty only the pleasing arrangement of form and color. Both were doorways to the divine. Both were lenses through which the soul could glimpse its own infinite nature.

From his earliest writings, Emerson spoke of love in tones that carried both tenderness and grandeur. The loss of his young wife Ellen had shown him how love pierces the heart with grief, yet also how it reveals depths of being that cannot be destroyed. To love is to be exposed, to be vulnerable, to feel one's life intertwined with another's. And when loss comes, as it inevitably does, one feels both the fragility of existence and the endurance of the bond. For Emerson, love was a paradox: it wounds and it heals, it binds and it frees, it teaches us that the soul's truest life is never solitary.

In his essay *Love* he described the experience of attraction as the soul recognizing itself in another form. "The lover seeks in marriage his own, the complement of his being." Love, he insisted, is not possession but recognition — a glimpse of the

Oversoul shining through another face, another voice, another gesture. It is the moment when separateness dissolves into communion, when two lives, while remaining distinct, discover themselves part of one life.

This recognition gave to Emerson's friendships their intensity, but it also shaped his broader understanding of human community. Love is not confined to romance or friendship; it is the underlying law of existence. It is the gravity of the soul, drawing beings together, holding creation in a web of communion. "Love is our highest word," he wrote, because it names not only human affection but the unity of all with all.

If love is the inward experience of unity, beauty is its outward expression. Emerson saw beauty as the form in which spirit reveals itself to the senses. A sunset, a face, a melody, a work of art — each becomes beautiful when it embodies the harmony of the Oversoul. Beauty awakens in us a recognition of wholeness. It is not mere ornament, not accidental pleasure, but revelation. In beauty, the finite hints at the infinite.

Walking in the woods of Concord, Emerson often paused at the sight of light filtering through leaves, or the delicate curve of a wildflower, or the expansive horizon of sky. These were not trivial charms to him; they were sacraments. Each shimmer of beauty was a window through which eternity looked into time. To be moved by beauty was, for Emerson, to feel the Oversoul pressing upon the heart.

He extended this to art. The poet, the painter, the musician — all are interpreters of beauty, channels through which spirit speaks. But the truest art is not artifice; it is fidelity to inspiration. The artist does not impose form but receives it, allows the Oversoul to shape expression. Thus art, at its highest, is not entertainment but revelation. It shows us ourselves transfigured, ourselves radiant with the eternal.

The "transparent eyeball" passage in *Nature* gathers love and beauty into one image. Emerson describes himself standing in solitude, head uplifted into infinite space, all mean egotism vanished, seeing all. He becomes pure perception, transparent, allowing the world to flow through him without obstruction. In that state, love and beauty are one: the love of being itself, the beauty of the whole, the recognition that subject and object are not two but one life.

This image has puzzled readers, sometimes even invited ridicule. What does it mean to become a transparent eyeball? Yet for Emerson it was the most natural metaphor for mystical perception. When the ego dissolves, the eye becomes not a barrier but a window, transparent to the divine light. To see in this way is to love without possessiveness, to perceive beauty without clinging, to recognize the Oversoul in every form.

Emerson was not naïve. He knew that love can become distorted into jealousy, that beauty can be commodified into vanity. He warned against mistaking appearances for essence. True love and true beauty arise only when grounded in the soul's recognition of unity. Without that grounding, they become distractions; with it, they become revelations.

In his own life, Emerson practiced a reverence for beauty in small things. Guests at his Concord home remembered vases of fresh flowers, carefully arranged not for display but for quiet delight. He walked daily in fields and forests, attentive to subtle changes of season, to the shifting hues of sky. He quoted lines of poetry, cherished music, and encouraged artists and writers around him. Beauty was not luxury but nourishment, a daily bread of the spirit.

Love, too, permeated his life, though not always in conventional forms. His second marriage to Lydia Jackson, whom he affectionately called

Lidian, was steady and supportive, though at times marked by difference in temperament. With friends, with students, with correspondents across the Atlantic, he poured out affection in letters that reveal both warmth and depth. To each he sought to offer not flattery but recognition, the assurance that the soul is seen and valued.

The intertwining of love and beauty in Emerson's thought points toward his larger vision: that life, in its essence, is not harsh or meaningless, but radiant. The world, when seen truly, is charged with beauty, and the soul, when awakened, responds with love. Together they dissolve isolation, transfigure sorrow, and open the heart to the infinite.

To live as Emerson did is to cultivate that transparent eye, to let oneself be pierced by beauty, to let love flow freely without fear, to recognize in every face and every flower the presence of the Oversoul. It is to walk in the world not as a consumer of pleasures but as a worshiper in a vast temple, where every beam of light and every gesture of kindness is a hymn of the divine.

Thus Emerson's wisdom on love and beauty is not sentimental but sacramental. It is not the romance of novels or the prettiness of surfaces, but the deep recognition that love is the law of being and beauty its language. To awaken to them is to awaken to the divine.

## Circles: The Endless Flow of Becoming

In January 1841, in the first series of his published *Essays,* Emerson offered a short but arresting meditation entitled *Circles*. Among all his works, this one perhaps most purely embodies his vision of life as ceaseless transformation. It is not one of his most quoted pieces, yet it remains central to understanding his philosophy. For in it he gave form to his intuition that existence itself is a series of circles endlessly expanding, each horizon yielding to a larger one, each seeming completion opening into new beginnings.

"The eye," he wrote, "is the first circle; the horizon which it forms is the second; and throughout nature this primary figure is repeated without end." He saw circles everywhere: in the ripple spreading across water, in the seasons turning, in the structures of plants, in the orbits of planets. But more than geometry, the circle for him was a symbol of spiritual law. Human life, too, moves in circles — patterns of thought, cycles of growth, expansions of consciousness. To live is to be drawn ever outward, to transcend what was once sufficient, to be called to new horizons.

This vision was born of Emerson's own experience. Again and again in his life, what had seemed final dissolved into transition. He had become a minister, and then resigned. He had married, and then been bereaved. He had sought truth in Europe, and then returned to find it in Concord's fields. Each time he felt the circle close, a new one opened. Loss became expansion; endings became beginnings. The philosophy of *Circles* was not an abstract speculation but a distillation of his lived pattern: life as perpetual becoming.

Emerson urged his readers to accept this law with courage. Most people, he warned, cling to fixed forms — doctrines, habits, reputations — fearing the dissolution of what they know. But to cling is to resist life itself, for the very essence of life is change. "People wish to be settled," he declared, "only as far as they are unsettled is there any hope for them." The words strike like thunder: it is not stability but openness to change that nourishes the soul. To live is to be unsettled, to allow the circle to widen, to trust that the next horizon holds new light.

The essay is filled with images of expansion. Emerson compares human thought to a series of concentric circles, each idea eventually encompassed by a larger one. What seems ultimate today will appear partial tomorrow. What we believe to be absolute will one day be revealed as relative, and a broader truth will dawn. This recognition requires humility: no creed, no philosophy, no self-image is final. Each must yield to growth.

In this light, Emerson's call to self-reliance acquires new depth. To trust oneself is not to cling to one's past assertions but to remain faithful to the inner movement of becoming. Fidelity to self means openness to transformation. "Speak what you think today in hard words," he had written in *Self-Reliance,* "and tomorrow speak what tomorrow thinks in hard words again, though it contradict every thing you said today." This is the law of circles: truth is not static but dynamic, not a possession but a living flow.

The spiritual implications are profound. If the Oversoul is the eternal unity, then our experience of it must be ever-deepening. Each glimpse is partial, each insight provisional, each vision awaiting a greater. Religion, philosophy, art — all are circles within circles, expanding toward infinity. To mistake any circle for the whole is idolatry; to embrace the expansion is wisdom.

Emerson himself embodied this expansion in his career. He began as a minister in the church, then became a minister without church, then a lecturer to the nation, then a sage whose influence extended beyond his own time. Each role was true, each was fulfilled, and each was transcended. The circle widened. Even his style reveals this movement: his essays rarely argue in linear fashion; they move in orbits, spiraling around a theme, approaching truth by ever-widening arcs.

To live by circles is also to live by trust. For the dissolution of the old circle can feel like death. When belief collapses, when vocation ends, when love is lost, one stands in emptiness. Emerson knew this intimately. Yet he discovered that beyond the collapse lies a wider horizon. "Our life is an apprenticeship to the truth," he wrote, "that around every circle another can be drawn." To trust this law is to face loss with courage, to meet uncertainty with openness, to recognize that the very groundlessness of life is the path to growth.

The image of circles also reveals Emerson's quiet critique of finality in theology and philosophy. Systems that claim absolute completion, he suggested, are illusions. Every system is provisional, every doctrine partial. Even his own writings are but circles destined to be encompassed. He invites his readers not to cling to his words but to use them as stepping stones, to move beyond him as he moved beyond his teachers. "The new position of the advancing man has all the powers of the old, yet has them all new." Thus even Emerson himself must be transcended.

In Concord, walking by Walden Pond or through the orchards, he often saw the circle embodied in nature. The seasons turning, spring rising from winter's death, autumn returning into quiet, showed him the rhythm of renewal. The growth of plants, the orbit of the moon, the ripple of water when a stone is cast — each testified to the same law. Nature became his teacher of expansion, showing that nothing is static, everything flows.

For those who heard him lecture, the message could be unsettling. He seemed to undermine certainty, to dissolve the comfort of fixed beliefs. Yet many also found in it liberation, a sense that life is richer than dogma, more spacious than creed. Emerson did not demand that one abandon faith but that one hold it lightly, open to greater light. The circle will always widen.

In the end, *Circles* is one of Emerson's most daring affirmations. It calls us to embrace impermanence not as loss but as law, to see in every ending the beginning of a larger horizon, to live not in fear of change but in reverence for becoming. To awaken to this truth is to live with a serenity that does not cling, with a courage that welcomes the unknown, with a wisdom that sees the eternal in the very movement of time.

Thus Emerson's vision of circles is not merely metaphor but invitation: to step into the flow of life, to let each circle widen into the next, to trust that the Oversoul itself is the infinite horizon toward which all circles expand.

## The Poet: Language, Imagination, and the World Made Anew

In 1844, Emerson published an essay that bore a title both simple and audacious: *The Poet*. In it he sought to define not merely the craft of verse but the very role of the creative spirit in human life. The poet, for Emerson, was not a mere versifier arranging words into pleasing rhythm, nor a decorative artist weaving ornament for leisure. The poet was a prophet, a revealer, one who sees freshly and names the world anew. Through the poet's vision, language itself is redeemed, and reality is disclosed in its divine radiance.

"Poets are thus liberating gods," he declared. They free us from the prison of habit, from the dead weight of conventional speech, from the dullness that comes when words no longer burn with meaning. To Emerson, language was not neutral. Words were living symbols, born originally from the immediate contact of mind with nature. But over time, words decay; they lose their freshness, becoming mere counters of exchange. The task of the poet is to restore their vitality, to reconnect them to the living source, to make us see the world again as if for the first time.

In this vision, the poet becomes the seer of the Oversoul. Where most pass through life blinded by custom, the poet perceives the eternal gleaming in the transient, the infinite shimmering in the finite. He or she speaks not from calculation but from inspiration, from that place where intuition and imagination merge. "The poet is representative," Emerson wrote, "he stands among partial men for the complete man, and apprises us not of his wealth, but of the commonwealth." The poet's voice is never merely private; it is the voice of the whole, given shape through an individual tongue.

This essay, though speaking of "the poet," was also Emerson's veiled declaration of his own vocation. He had once stood in pulpits, then at lecterns, speaking as minister and lecturer. But in truth, his deepest identity was that of a poet, not confined to verse but living in prose that burns with cadence and imagery. His sentences were not arguments but incantations, their power lying not in logical sequence but in luminous suggestion. "Poetry must be as new as foam, and as old as the rock," he insisted — and in his own essays, he sought to enact that very fusion.

Yet Emerson also recognized the scarcity of true poets. He longed for an American bard who would give voice to the spirit of the new land, who would name its rivers and forests, who would sing the Oversoul in an accent native to the soil. He saw glimpses of this possibility in his contemporaries, but it was only with Whitman's *Leaves of Grass,* published a decade later, that Emerson felt the arrival of what he had envisioned. In his famous letter to Whitman, he greeted the book as "the most extraordinary piece of wit and wisdom that America has yet contributed." Whitman had embodied the very figure Emerson had prophesied: a poet whose language broke conventions and revealed the divinity of common life.

What Emerson sought in the poet was imagination, that power to see beyond surfaces into essences. Imagination was, for him, the faculty by which the Oversoul becomes visible, the bridge between sense and spirit. Without imagination, life shrinks into routine; with it, every object becomes emblematic, every fact symbolic. The poet thus becomes not only artist but prophet, reminding humanity that reality is never exhausted by appearances.

But poetry, as Emerson conceived it, was not confined to literature. Anyone who speaks freshly, who names truth from immediate experience, participates in the poetic vocation. The farmer who sees the land with reverence, the mother who names her child with love, the thinker who coins a phrase that reveals a hidden truth — all are poets. Poetry is less a profession than a mode of perception, a way of living attuned to the divine radiance in the ordinary.

In Concord, Emerson cultivated this poetic vision daily. He gathered phrases in his journals, noting sudden flashes of thought, striking images, sentences that came to him as if dictated by a larger mind. Later he would polish them into essays, but their origin lay in those moments of inspiration when words seemed to descend upon him. He trusted these moments, believed them to be gifts of the Oversoul, signs that language still carried divine electricity.

The poet's task, Emerson insisted, is not to escape the world but to redeem it. Beauty is not elsewhere, in some distant heaven; it is here, awaiting recognition. The poet teaches us to see the miraculous in the commonplace: the holiness of a blade of grass, the grandeur of a drop of dew. "The true poet," he wrote, "animates nature with his own soul, and the world glows again with a beauty which it had lost." Through poetry, creation is continually renewed.

There was also a democratic impulse in Emerson's vision. He believed that America, young and unburdened by old hierarchies, was fertile soil for poetic revelation. Every person, he suggested, carries within the seed of poetry, the capacity to perceive freshly and speak truly. The poet is not a distant genius but a representative, showing others what they too can see. In this way, Emerson's poetics aligns with his broader philosophy of self-reliance: trust your perception, speak your truth, let the Oversoul flow through your words.

Still, he was clear about the demands of the calling. True poetry requires not only inspiration but discipline, not only vision but fidelity. The poet must cultivate solitude, must listen inwardly, must be faithful to the moment of inspiration and not betray it by compromise. He must risk misunderstanding, must endure isolation, must speak even when society scoffs. For the poet's loyalty is not to applause but to truth.

Thus Emerson, in writing *The Poet,* was also shaping the contours of his own life. He lived as one who believed that words matter, that language is a sacred trust, that imagination is the bridge between man and the divine. His essays, though in prose, are suffused with the rhythms of poetry, their sentences glowing like lines of verse, their cadences carrying the hush of revelation. He may not have been America's national bard in verse, but he was its great poetic seer in prose.

To read Emerson on the poet is to be reminded that our deepest task is not merely to survive, nor even to prosper, but to see. To see freshly, to name truthfully, to let language be born again in our mouths — this is the vocation of every soul. In that act, the world is made new, shimmering once more with the light of the Oversoul.

## America Awakening: The Intellectual Climate of the 1830s and 1840s

To understand Emerson's rise and the resonance of his message, one must enter the atmosphere of America in the 1830s and 1840s — a young republic awakening to its own identity, restless, experimental, filled with energy yet still haunted by the shadows of the Old World. This was the climate in which Emerson's voice found its audience, the soil in which Transcendentalism took root. Without that context, one risks hearing his essays as solitary meditations, when in truth they were part of a larger cultural tide, a collective searching for meaning.

The United States was scarcely sixty years removed from independence, and though politically free, culturally it still looked across the Atlantic for models. Universities revered European philosophy, churches carried the weight of inherited doctrines, artists imitated British forms, intellectuals measured themselves by continental standards. Yet the land itself, vast and untamed, whispered of new possibilities. Forests stretched beyond imagining, rivers cut through wilderness, frontiers beckoned westward. The contradiction was stark: a nation materially expansive yet spiritually tethered to

Europe. Emerson was among the first to declare that America must think with its own mind, speak with its own voice, find divinity in its own soil.

The intellectual climate was shaped by several converging forces. Unitarianism, with its emphasis on reason, benevolence, and moral progress, had become the religion of Boston elites. It rejected Calvinist severity, affirming instead a rational and humane God. Emerson, raised within its orbit, absorbed its spirit of liberalism but soon found it insufficient. For all its reasonableness, it lacked fire, lacked the immediacy of revelation. He longed for a religion of experience, not doctrine — a longing that would lead to the Divinity School Address.

At the same time, the Second Great Awakening swept through the country with revivalist fervor. Camp meetings, ecstatic conversions, preachers thundering about salvation and damnation — this was a religion of passion rather than reason, electrifying the hearts of common folk. Emerson respected its energy but found its theology crude. Between the dry rationalism of Unitarianism and the emotional excesses of revivalism, he sought a third way: the path of inward intuition, of direct encounter with the divine in nature and soul.

Social reform was also stirring. The 1830s and 1840s were decades of ferment: abolitionists denounced slavery, women demanded rights, utopian communities sprang up with visions of equality and simplicity. The air was charged with experiment. Brook Farm, Fruitlands, Shaker villages — all embodied attempts to live differently, to embody ideals in social form. Though Emerson never fully joined these experiments, he sympathized with their spirit and supported many reformers. His own philosophy, emphasizing self-reliance and the Oversoul, provided an underpinning for the moral courage of abolitionists and feminists alike.

Literature, too, was in the midst of awakening. Washington Irving and James Fenimore Cooper had begun to sketch an American literature, but it was Emerson, Thoreau, Hawthorne, and later Whitman who would give it voice of depth. In Emerson's time, there was a hunger for words that matched the landscapes of America, for a language not borrowed but native. His essays, filled with images of forests and rivers, of stars and seasons, answered that hunger. They declared that America need not mimic Europe; it could speak from its own experience, with its own metaphors, its own authority.

The intellectual climate was also influenced by the first trickles of Eastern thought reaching American shores. Translations of the Bhagavad Gita, the Upanishads, Confucian Analects, and Buddhist sutras began to circulate among scholars. Emerson, always eager for wisdom from beyond the familiar, devoured these texts. They confirmed his intuition that truth is universal, that revelation is not confined to Christianity. These sources nourished his conception of the Oversoul and broadened the horizons of Transcendentalism, giving it a global dimension rare for its time.

Meanwhile, the social realities of the era pressed upon conscience. Slavery, entrenched in the South and tolerated in the North, loomed as a moral crisis. Industrialization was beginning to transform labor, cities were growing, immigrants were arriving, Native peoples were being displaced. Amid these changes, many Americans felt both exhilaration and unease. Emerson's voice, serene yet radical, provided orientation: trust yourself, trust nature, trust the Oversoul. In a world of upheaval, his philosophy offered not escape but grounding.

The Concord circle — Emerson, Thoreau, Margaret Fuller, Bronson Alcott, Theodore Parker, and others — became the heart of this intellectual ferment. They met in parlors and libraries, walked through meadows, debated late into the night. Their conversations were not idle; they were experiments in thought, attempts to articulate a new vision of human possibility. Concord, a small town, became for a time the intellectual capital of America, its orchards and ponds charged with ideas that would reverberate across centuries.

What set Emerson apart within this climate was not only his ideas but his manner. Others argued; he evoked. Others laid out systems; he scattered sparks. His essays did not read like philosophy in the European sense, but like oracles, fragments of vision, aphorisms that invited meditation. In a culture hungry for new beginnings, this style resonated. It felt fresh, native, unborrowed. Emerson was not another scholastic voice; he was America speaking itself into being.

The 1830s and 1840s were decades of awakening — religious, social, literary, intellectual. Emerson stood at their center, not as commander but as catalyst, the one who gave voice to the aspirations of a restless generation. He told America that its landscapes were scripture, its individuals divine, its destiny not to imitate but to create. He summoned it to self-reliance, to unity, to beauty.

In his words, the young nation began to recognize its own soul.

## Transcendentalism and Its Circle: Thoreau, Margaret Fuller, and the Concord Gatherings

Though Emerson often walked alone, his thought did not blossom in isolation. Around him gathered a constellation of seekers who, together, gave shape and energy to what would be called Transcendentalism. The name itself was never fully embraced by those within the circle — it was more a label imposed from without, borrowed from German philosophy, softened through English intermediaries, and adapted by American journalists to describe a movement that defied precise definition. But whatever one calls it, in Concord and Boston during the 1830s and 1840s a group of men and women began meeting, conversing, and writing in ways that would alter the course of American intellectual and literary life. Emerson stood at the center of this circle, not as master but as magnet, drawing others into orbit by the quiet force of his presence.

Among them, Henry David Thoreau was perhaps the most intimate and enduring. Born in Concord in 1817, Thoreau grew up in the very soil Emerson had come to inhabit. When the two first met, Emerson was already the town's most notable resident, while Thoreau was a young Harvard graduate searching for his vocation. Emerson recognized in him a kindred spirit, a fierce independence tempered by a contemplative soul. He invited Thoreau into his home, offered him access to his library, encouraged his writing. For a time, Thoreau even lived under Emerson's roof, tending the garden and helping with household tasks, while absorbing from his mentor a sense of life lived in fidelity to conscience.

Yet their friendship was not one of easy hierarchy. Thoreau, with his uncompromising honesty and love of solitude, could not be a disciple in the conventional sense. He took Emerson's philosophy and radicalized it, carrying self-reliance into the woods of Walden Pond, testing simplicity not in theory but in practice. Emerson admired his courage, though at times he found Thoreau prickly, too severe in judgment. Still, the bond between them endured, each serving as mirror to the other: Emerson the expansive sage, Thoreau the ascetic experimenter. Together they embodied two faces of Transcendentalism — the eloquence of vision and the discipline of practice.

If Thoreau gave the movement its embodiment in nature, Margaret Fuller gave it voice in society. Brilliant, restless, fiercely intelligent, Fuller was a force of nature in her own right. She joined the Emersonian circle not as a subordinate but as an equal, often as its sharpest critic. In the parlors of Boston, she led the famous "Conversations" for women, gatherings in which intellectual exchange was cultivated as a form of liberation. She pushed Transcendentalism beyond the solitary soul toward the emancipation of women, toward social reform and political action.

Emerson admired her intellect, calling her "the greatest woman of the age," though their relationship was not without friction. Fuller's intensity sometimes clashed with his serenity, her demand for engagement sometimes unsettled his preference for contemplation. Yet he respected her deeply, and their dialogue enriched them both. Her book *Woman in the Nineteenth Century* became one of the foundational texts of American feminism, its seeds nourished by the soil of Emersonian thought yet flowering into her own distinct vision.

Then there was Amos Bronson Alcott, eccentric, impractical, endlessly speculative. A visionary educator, he founded schools that emphasized intuition and moral development over rote learning. His ideas were often too radical for the public, and he suffered repeated failures, yet Emerson remained loyal, seeing in Alcott a kind of prophetic innocence. Alcott's conversations in Concord parlors became legendary, weaving philosophy, theology, and pedagogy into daring experiments of thought. Though mocked by some as fanciful, he contributed to the ferment of ideas that made the Transcendentalist circle more than a literary club — it was a laboratory of the spirit.

The gatherings themselves — often called the Transcendental Club, though informality was their hallmark — took place in Boston parlors and Concord living rooms. There was no membership list, no creed, no hierarchy. Instead, there were conversations: free, searching, often tumultuous. Participants included Theodore Parker, a Unitarian minister whose sermons thundered against slavery and who carried Emerson's vision into the arena of social reform. There was Orestes Brownson, whose restless journey carried him from Transcendentalist enthusiasm to Roman Catholic conversion, leaving behind essays that reveal both the brilliance and instability of his mind. There was Jones Very, a mystic poet whose visions led him to declare himself divinely inspired, unsettling even his friends. The circle was porous, experimental, alive.

What bound them was less agreement than aspiration. Each sought to transcend the limitations of inherited forms, to discover a more immediate relation to truth. Some emphasized intuition, others social reform, others education, others poetry. Yet beneath the diversity lay a shared conviction: that the soul is divine, that nature is revelation, that truth is not past but present. Emerson, with his calm radiance, provided the axis around which this restless energy revolved.

The Concord gatherings extended beyond conversation into experiment. Brook Farm, founded in 1841 near Boston, embodied the attempt to live Transcendentalist ideals in community. There, intellectuals and farmers labored side by side, seeking harmony between work and spirit. Emerson visited, supported its aims, but remained cautious; he sensed the impracticality, the difficulty of embodying vision in economic life. Brook Farm eventually collapsed, but its existence testified to the urgency of the age, the longing to incarnate ideals.

Transcendentalism, for all its loftiness, was not confined to abstraction. Its members were engaged in the pressing issues of their time: abolition, women's rights, education, the reform of labor. Emerson himself, though often preferring to speak of spirit rather than politics, increasingly gave his voice to the cause of anti-slavery. Fuller carried her vision into journalism, even into the revolutionary struggles of Italy. Parker risked his pulpit to denounce injustice. The circle was porous to the world, its ideas flowing into action.

Yet the true power of the movement lay in its interiority. It gave individuals permission to trust themselves, to seek truth beyond institutions, to live in harmony with nature, to speak in fresh language. It was less a school of doctrine than a contagion of courage, a permission granted to souls to awaken. And in that awakening, literature flourished: Thoreau's *Walden*, Fuller's *Woman in the Nineteenth Century*, Parker's sermons, Alcott's pedagogical experiments — all bore the imprint of the circle.

Looking back, one sees the Concord gatherings not as a formal movement but as a moment — a brief flowering of intellectual and spiritual intensity in a small New England town. The orchards, the meadows, the ponds of Concord became charged with meanings that still echo. Visitors remarked on the atmosphere: the sense that in Emerson's parlor, or walking with Thoreau by Walden, or listening to Fuller's fierce eloquence, one was touching the pulse of something larger than themselves.

Emerson himself remained at the center, but never as dictator. He listened more than he spoke, encouraged more than he directed. His gift was to create space where others could find their own voices. He was the sun around which the planets orbited, yet he insisted that each must shine with its own light. The circle, in its diversity and turbulence, reflected his own philosophy: individuality and unity, self-reliance and communion, circles widening into circles.

Thus Transcendentalism was less a creed than a climate, less a doctrine than a spirit. It was the air breathed in Concord in those years, the ferment of minds daring to trust intuition, to revere nature, to affirm the divinity of the soul. Its circle, gathered around Emerson, became the seedbed of a distinctly American philosophy and literature, a testament that even in a small village, with simple houses and modest means, the Oversoul could speak with a voice that would echo across the world.

## Trials of the Spirit: Grief, Illness, and the Loss of a Child

The philosophy Emerson offered to the world was not born in ease, nor was it the tranquil speculation of a man untouched by sorrow. Beneath the serene cadences of his prose lies the echo of griefs that shaped him, losses that burned away complacency and left him standing in the stark presence of impermanence. Among these, none cut more deeply than the death of his firstborn son, Waldo. That trial, searing and unrelenting, tested the very core of his convictions and gave his thought the gravity that distinguishes lived wisdom from mere speculation.

Waldo was born in 1836, the year *Nature* was published — a child of promise arriving as the philosophy of promise was being declared. Emerson loved him with a tenderness that those who knew him sometimes found surprising, for the sage of Concord, dignified and reserved, revealed in the presence of his son an unguarded joy. The boy was bright, lively, filled with questions, a companion on his father's walks, a presence in the study, a spark in the household. Emerson saw in him not only filial love but the embodiment of innocence, the Oversoul shining through a child's laughter.

But in January 1842, scarlet fever swept through the Concord household. The illness came swiftly, with its fever and delirium, leaving little room for hope. Within days, young Waldo, just five years old, was gone. Emerson, who had known the grief of losing a father in childhood and a wife in early manhood, now faced the most piercing of losses: the death of a child, a piece of himself torn away. He stood by the small grave in Concord, snow falling, his heart hollowed.

His journals from those days reveal a man stripped bare. "The blow I cannot yet realize," he wrote. "The morning of the 28th of January was a calamity." In another entry he confessed, "I cannot get it near enough to compare it with thoughts. Death of a boy. The only event that ever touches me as this does." These lines carry none of the serene confidence of his published essays; they reveal raw grief, bewilderment, the silence of a father undone.

And yet, slowly, Emerson's philosophy began to engage the loss. He turned to the vision of the Oversoul, to the conviction that no soul is lost, that all are gathered into the eternal. He wrote of Waldo: "The soul of this child is secure in God, in the Oversoul." Still, the words were not enough to quell the ache. His essay *Experience,* written in the wake of Waldo's death, is perhaps his most poignant, precisely because it bears the marks of wrestling with grief. In it he confesses that sorrow seems to fall upon us like a dream, dulled by the very inability of our faculties to absorb it fully. "The lords of life, the lords of life," he wrote, "I saw them pass, in their own guise, like and unlike, portly and grim, use and surprise, surface and dream, succession swift, and spectral wrong, temper of the will, desire and wrong, glimpse of the true, yet the longing, and the sting of the grief remains."

*Experience* is not an essay of resolution but of struggle. Emerson admits that grief did not yield the spiritual fruit he expected, that the pain remained stubborn, untransformed. He even wrote, with chilling candor, "I grieve that grief can teach me nothing." Such words may sound like failure, but in truth they mark his honesty: even the sage cannot transmute every sorrow into serenity. Sometimes grief resists philosophy. Sometimes it simply abides, a weight the soul must carry.

Illness, too, marked his household. Other children fell ill; his wife Lidian often struggled with fragile health. Emerson himself, though outwardly robust in spirit, carried bouts of weakness, failing eyesight, and exhaustion from his relentless lecturing schedule. These bodily trials reminded him that the soul's reliance cannot erase the body's vulnerability. He saw clearly that to be human is to live in a fragile vessel, always exposed to suffering.

Yet rather than turning him toward despair, these trials deepened his conviction that the soul's essence is untouched. If grief showed him the fragility of human joy, the Oversoul showed him the permanence of divine unity. If illness revealed the limits of strength, self-reliance reminded him that the divine spark remains even when flesh falters. Thus Emerson's philosophy is not denial of suffering but insistence that suffering is not ultimate.

The loss of Waldo also altered the tone of his thought. Before, he had spoken of nature with unalloyed joy, of self-reliance with youthful audacity. Afterward, there is a gravity, a recognition of shadow. His later works carry a depth born of mourning. Readers sometimes sense a coolness, even detachment, in his later style — but beneath it lies the scar of grief, the wisdom of one who has walked through fire.

For Emerson, trials of the spirit were not obstacles but passages. Each loss drew him further from reliance on circumstance into reliance on the eternal. Each illness reminded him that body and world are transient, while spirit endures. Each grief became, however unwillingly, a teacher of humility, of compassion, of depth.

Visitors to Emerson's Concord home after Waldo's death remarked on his composure. He did not wear grief on his sleeve; he carried it inwardly, with a dignity that seemed both strength and wound. He continued to lecture, to write, to converse with friends. But those who looked closely saw that something had changed: the transparency of joy was tempered by shadow, the serenity deepened by sorrow.

And yet, it was precisely this that gave his words their enduring resonance. Readers sensed that Emerson did not speak from ivory towers but from the valley of grief. His assurance of the Oversoul was not easy optimism but hard-won conviction. His call to self-reliance was not the boast of privilege but the counsel of one who had lost and yet endured.

Thus the trials of the spirit, culminating in the loss of his child, shaped Emerson's philosophy into lived wisdom. They gave weight to his words, depth to his vision, compassion to his counsel. They showed that the transparent eyeball sees not only beauty but also mortality, not only light but also shadow — and yet finds in both the radiance of the eternal.

## Politics of Conscience: Slavery, Abolition, and the Voice of Justice

For much of his life, Emerson preferred to dwell in the realm of ideas, in nature, in the quiet radiance of spiritual intuition. He was by temperament not a political agitator but a contemplative, one who trusted that the transformation of the soul was the deepest source of social renewal. Yet no life lived with integrity can remain untouched by the great injustices of its age, and for Emerson that injustice was slavery. In the 1830s and 1840s, as the United States expanded westward and the moral crisis of human bondage deepened, Emerson found himself compelled to give his voice to conscience, to enter the fray not as partisan but as prophet.

At first, he hesitated. The radical abolitionists, led by William Lloyd Garrison, thundered from pulpits and presses with uncompromising zeal. Emerson admired their moral clarity but recoiled from their harshness, their refusal of nuance, their relentless denunciations. He was, by disposition, a man of balance, of serenity. He feared that anger, even when righteous, could blind rather than illumine. And yet, as the 1840s wore on and the Fugitive Slave Act of 1850 placed the cruelty of slavery at New England's doorstep, his silence grew untenable. Conscience would not let him rest.

His first public addresses on slavery were cautious, couched in the language of general principles. He spoke of liberty, of the dignity of man, of the contradiction between the republic's founding ideals and the practice of bondage. But as the years passed, his tone sharpened. In 1844, at Concord, he declared with rare passion: "We cannot have one law for the white man, another for the black. Liberty is the right of all men." The audience, accustomed to Emerson's philosophical calm, heard in these words the tremor of moral fire.

The passage of the Fugitive Slave Act in 1850, which required citizens of free states to aid in the capture of escaped slaves, brought the issue to his own town. Fugitive men and women, who had sought shelter in the North, could now be seized from their homes and dragged back into bondage. Emerson, usually gentle in tone, erupted in outrage. He called the law "a filthy enactment" and urged his neighbors to resist it. "I will not obey it," he told an audience in Concord, "by God's help, I will not obey it." In that defiance, Emerson revealed that self-reliance and moral law were one: fidelity to conscience demanded disobedience to injustice.

It was not easy for him. He disliked conflict, shunned polemic, and cherished serenity. But slavery pierced through all such preference. The sight of human beings treated as property, of families torn apart, of men and women denied their humanity, compelled him to speak. His words may not have carried the fire of Garrison's, but they carried something quieter: the authority of a man who had long urged fidelity to the inner voice and now demonstrated it in public conscience.

Emerson also lent support to those on the front lines. He praised and encouraged Theodore Parker, the radical Unitarian minister whose pulpit became a platform for abolitionist thunder. He defended the memory of John Brown after his raid on Harpers Ferry, declaring that Brown had become a martyr of conscience, a man whose action, though condemned as criminal by many, revealed the depth of slavery's moral wound. Emerson, who so often celebrated peace, now found himself affirming the sacrifice of a man who had chosen violence for the sake of justice.

In these years, the philosopher of the Oversoul became also a citizen of conscience. He saw clearly that unity does not mean passivity, that love must sometimes take the form of resistance. If every soul is divine, then the denial of that divinity in others is the greatest blasphemy. Slavery was not only a social evil but a spiritual desecration, and Emerson could not remain silent before it.

Yet his contribution was distinct. He did not organize campaigns or publish abolitionist newspapers. His gift was language, and he used it to awaken the conscience of his listeners. His lectures on slavery, delivered across New England, appealed not to hatred of the South but to fidelity to principle. He reminded audiences that America's promise was liberty, that the nation's very soul was at stake. His calm, measured words carried moral weight precisely because they came from one not given to invective. In his quiet way, he helped shift the moral climate of the North.

This engagement revealed another dimension of his philosophy. Self-reliance, often misread as solitary independence, here showed itself as moral courage in public. The Oversoul, often perceived as mystical abstraction, here demanded justice for the enslaved. Nature, often celebrated as beauty, here became the measure of freedom, for just as no tree or river could be owned, so no soul could rightly be possessed. Emerson's politics of conscience was not separate from his philosophy but its extension into the life of his nation.

The Civil War, when it came, filled him with sorrow and inevitability. He supported the Union cause, gave lectures to raise morale, visited camps, and urged emancipation as the war's true purpose. He rejoiced when Lincoln issued the Emancipation Proclamation, seeing in it a step toward the alignment of America with its own ideals. Yet he mourned the bloodshed, the terrible price of justice delayed. For Emerson, the war was both tragedy and necessity, the circle of history widening through fire.

When slavery was finally abolished, Emerson did not declare triumph. He knew that the deeper work of justice remained, that freedom on paper must be embodied in lives. But he took solace in knowing that conscience had prevailed, that the Oversoul had spoken through the struggle of a people, that America, however bloodied, had moved closer to its promise.

Thus Emerson, reluctant prophet of politics, became in the end a voice of justice. He showed that philosophy cannot remain aloof from suffering, that spirituality divorced from conscience is hollow. His words on slavery may not have been the most radical of his age, but they carried the authority of one who lived by the principle he urged: trust the inner voice, even when it calls you into conflict.

For Emerson, politics was never about power but about principle, never about parties but about conscience. To stand against slavery was to affirm the Oversoul, to practice self-reliance, to live in harmony with truth. In that stand, Emerson revealed that the sage of Concord was not only a poet of spirit but a citizen of justice, one whose voice, calm yet unwavering, joined the chorus that made freedom ring.

## England and the Old World Revisited: Lectures Abroad and Reflections on Civilization

In 1847, fifteen years after his first European journey, Emerson once more crossed the Atlantic. He had left America this time not as a bereaved young minister seeking bearings, but as a recognized voice, a lecturer whose essays were beginning to circulate, a thinker whose fame had spread beyond Concord. If his first journey had been an apprenticeship, his second was a visitation: the New World sage returning to the Old World, carrying with him not only curiosity but also a mirror in which Europe might see itself anew.

England received him with curiosity. By now, his essays had reached British readers, and some critics had already remarked upon the freshness of this American mind, half poet, half philosopher. Invitations to lecture awaited him, and audiences came to hear what this man from across the sea might say. He spoke in Manchester, Liverpool, London, Edinburgh, and other cities, his calm cadence carrying across halls filled with merchants, students, and men of letters.

His subject was often "Representative Men," the series of lectures that would later become one of his major books. In them he portrayed history through the lens of great figures — Plato, Montaigne, Shakespeare, Napoleon, Goethe — each embodying a principle, each a type of human possibility. To the English audiences, hungry for portraits of genius, his words offered both familiarity and surprise. He praised their Shakespeare with reverence but insisted that the task of every nation is not only to revere but to create, to bring forth new voices rather than bow before old monuments.

What struck Emerson most was not only the individuals he met but the social landscape. England impressed him with its power, its industry, its vast wealth. He toured factories and railroads, saw the machinery of industrialization transforming society at a pace unimaginable in Concord. He admired the energy, the efficiency, the sheer force of will. Yet he also saw the cost: the smoke, the squalor, the rigid class divisions, the alienation of labor. Civilization, he concluded, is always two-sided: it refines and it corrodes, it creates abundance and it breeds inequality. His reflections would eventually find form in the book *English Traits,* published in 1856, a blend of admiration and critique, observation and philosophy.

He noted, too, the character of the English people — their practicality, their respect for institutions, their discipline. He admired their steadiness, their courage, their devotion to law. But he also saw their limitations: a certain insularity, a conservatism of mind, a suspicion of the new. To Emerson, America's task was not to imitate England but to balance its virtues with a fresher openness, to avoid being weighed down by tradition while learning from its strengths.

One of the most significant personal encounters of this journey was his reunion with Thomas Carlyle. The two had corresponded faithfully since their first meeting in Scotland years earlier, their letters crossing the ocean like lifelines between kindred spirits. In 1847, Emerson traveled to Carlyle's home at Chelsea, where the old friendship was renewed in person. Carlyle, stormy and irascible as ever, railed against democracy, against the follies of the age, against the "swarm of small men" replacing heroes. Emerson, calm and serene, listened, reflected, and replied with gentleness. Their differences were clear — Carlyle suspicious of popular movements, Emerson trusting in the dignity of the individual soul — yet the bond endured. Each saw in the other a mirror of seriousness, of fidelity to conscience, even if their conclusions diverged.

The lectures in England revealed Emerson's peculiar power. He was not a dramatic orator; his voice was measured, his gestures minimal. Yet his words carried weight. Audiences remarked on the way he seemed to speak less to their intellect than to their conscience, less to argue than to awaken. Even in industrial cities, among men hardened by commerce, his words about the Oversoul, about the dignity of the individual, about the sanctity of nature, struck chords. He was, as one listener put it, "a man who made you feel the air was larger around you."

From England, he traveled briefly to France, to Italy again, and to other parts of the continent. But his gaze was always comparative, always asking: what does this reveal about civilization? In Paris he once more visited the Jardin des Plantes, renewing the wonder that had inspired him years earlier. In Rome he admired the ruins but reaffirmed his conviction that America must look to its own future, not live in the shadows of Europe's past. The Old World offered grandeur, but also decay; it offered heritage, but also burden.

When Emerson returned to Concord in 1848, he carried with him not only memories but insights that would shape his reflections for years to come. In *English Traits,* he crystallized his observations.

He praised the English for their independence, their love of liberty, their genius for practical organization. He critiqued them for their materialism, their rigidity, their obsession with wealth and rank. The book was received with interest on both sides of the Atlantic, though not without offense. Some English readers bristled at the American's judgments; some Americans thought him too generous. Yet the book remains one of the most penetrating portraits of a national character by an outsider.

More broadly, the second European journey affirmed Emerson's conviction that America's destiny was not to imitate but to create. Europe was old, rich in tradition but heavy with its weight. America was young, unburdened, still plastic. Its task was to bring forth a culture of its own, a philosophy and literature rooted in its landscapes, its democracy, its individuality. Emerson returned more convinced than ever that the divine speaks in the present, that revelation is not behind us but before us.

The experience also deepened his sense of civilization itself. He came to see civilization as a balance between material power and spiritual vitality. Industry, science, law — these are necessary, but they are not sufficient. Without imagination, without conscience, without reverence for nature and the soul, civilization collapses into mere mechanism. The true measure of a nation, Emerson concluded, is not its wealth or armies but the quality of its thought, the depth of its culture, the vitality of its spirit.

Thus the second European journey was not escape but mirror. Emerson saw in the Old World both what to emulate and what to transcend. He admired its strength, its discipline, its achievements, but he resolved that America must not become its copy. The New World must speak in its own tongue, must trust its own genius, must draw revelation from its own rivers and skies.

When he walked again through the woods of Concord after his return, he felt this more keenly. The grandeur of cathedrals, the ruins of empires, the sophistication of cities — all paled before the quiet sanctity of New England fields bathed in morning light. For Emerson, the Oversoul spoke there as clearly as in Rome or Paris, perhaps more clearly. The true civilization, he believed, would be born not in the imitation of the old but in the fidelity of the new, in men and women who trusted their own thought and lived in harmony with nature and conscience.

## Later Years: Memory, Forgetting, and the Quietude of Concord

The arc of Emerson's life, like one of his own circles, widened outward into fame and influence before curving inward again toward quietude. In his later years, he remained the Sage of Concord, the serene presence whose words had shaped a generation, but he also became a figure touched by frailty, his memory faltering, his speech hesitant, his once-fiery eloquence dimmed by the gentle fog of age. Yet even in decline, his life bore testimony to the truths he had proclaimed: that the soul is larger than circumstance, that serenity can coexist with loss, that the Oversoul shines through even when the faculties dim.

By the 1850s and 1860s, Emerson had reached the height of his reputation. His lectures drew crowds across the country; his essays circulated widely; his Concord home became a place of pilgrimage. He was invited to speak at Harvard again, after decades of unofficial banishment, and he did so with dignity, no bitterness in his tone. To young writers and thinkers he became a mentor, his very presence a benediction. Whitman sought his approval, Thoreau walked with him by Walden, reformers sought his counsel. Yet with the years came a shift. The sharp edge of his prose softened, his lectures became more repetitive, his thought less startling. Some noticed, some lamented, but Emerson himself seemed untroubled. He accepted the ebb as naturally as he had once embraced the flow.

The Civil War shook him, as it shook all of America. He supported the Union cause, lent his voice to abolition, and rejoiced in the emancipation of the enslaved. He eulogized Lincoln as a man of character, a leader whose greatness lay not in grandeur but in fidelity to conscience. Yet the war also deepened his sense of the tragic, the recognition that progress often exacts terrible costs. The circle of history, he saw, widens through fire as well as through light.

As the 1870s unfolded, memory began to slip from him. He would rise to lecture and lose his thread, pause in mid-sentence, struggle to recall a word. Audiences, once stirred by his oratory, now listened with tenderness, aware that they were witnessing not the decline of dignity but the passage of a life into its final season. In his Concord home, he sometimes wandered rooms in forgetfulness, yet his presence remained luminous. Visitors remarked that even when words failed, his gentleness, his calm, his gaze carried the same serenity as always.

In 1872, his house caught fire. Neighbors rushed to save books and manuscripts, carrying armloads of papers into the yard. Emerson, standing in the chill, wrapped in a cloak, watched with a quiet acceptance. He seemed less distraught than those around him, as though the loss of objects was of little matter compared to the enduring presence of spirit. Friends arranged for him to travel to Europe and Egypt while the house was repaired. He visited the Nile, gazed at pyramids, stood among ancient temples. Yet even there, in lands older than memory, he seemed more spectator than pilgrim, his mind no longer reaching outward but settling into inward quiet.

Returning to Concord, he entered the final years of life in a kind of twilight. Forgetfulness grew, and with it a detachment that was not despair but gentle fading. He would walk familiar paths, sometimes uncertain of names, but always attuned to the presence of nature. Flowers, trees, the changing sky — these remained his companions, constants even as memory dissolved. In these years, he embodied his own teaching that the Oversoul is not bound by intellect, that the soul's radiance persists even when faculties falter.

Family and friends cared for him tenderly. His wife Lidian, steadfast through decades, remained his anchor. His daughter Ellen became his companion and protector, guiding him when he faltered, preserving his dignity with quiet devotion. Neighbors in Concord treated him with reverence, not as a relic but as a presence. They saw in him not the decline of greatness but its transfiguration into simplicity.

On April 27, 1882, Emerson breathed his last. He was seventy-eight years old. His funeral, held in Concord, drew crowds from near and far. He was laid to rest in Sleepy Hollow Cemetery, on Author's Ridge, near Thoreau, Hawthorne, and the Alcotts. The spot became a place of pilgrimage, where admirers still come to leave flowers, stones, and words. The Sage of Concord had returned to the soil he loved, the soil he had taught others to see as scripture.

Looking back upon his later years, one sees not tragedy but fulfillment. Emerson had lived his philosophy: he had trusted himself, he had listened to nature, he had spoken what he saw. In age and decline, he trusted still, accepted still, saw still — even when memory failed, the Oversoul remained. His life closed not in despair but in quietude, like a circle returning to its center.

The lesson of his later years is perhaps the deepest of all. Greatness does not lie only in brilliance, in fiery eloquence, in bold declarations. It lies also in the ability to fade with dignity, to accept the diminishment of faculties while resting in the presence of spirit. Emerson's twilight teaches that the soul's essence is untouched by forgetfulness, that serenity can outlast memory, that the Oversoul shines even when words fail.

Thus the Sage of Concord, who had spoken so much of circles, ended his life within one more: the circle of rise and return, of eloquence and silence, of memory and forgetting, of individuality dissolving once more into the whole. In his quietude, he became again a transparent eyeball, nothing and everything, open to the infinite.

## Emerson's Legacy: Seeds Carried into Modern Thought and Literature

When Emerson was laid to rest on Author's Ridge in Concord, the body was buried, but the voice remained. His sentences — luminous, compact, suggestive — had entered the bloodstream of American thought. His presence lingered not only in the quiet streets of Concord but across a continent, across a century, across disciplines of philosophy, literature, and spirituality. Emerson's true legacy was not a school or a doctrine, for he founded none, but seeds: ideas scattered on fertile ground, germinating in minds and movements far beyond his lifetime.

In literature, the first great heir was Walt Whitman. When Whitman published *Leaves of Grass* in 1855, it was Emerson's voice that hailed it with enthusiasm. "I greet you at the beginning of a great career," he wrote in a private letter that Whitman, to Emerson's embarrassment, soon made public. Whitman was the poet Emerson had prophesied in his essay *The Poet*: a bard who spoke in a new American tongue, celebrating the body, democracy, the common man, the Oversoul shimmering in every blade of grass. Whitman's exuberant lines are unthinkable without

Emerson's permission to trust the inner light and to speak freshly of the world.

Thoreau, too, was his legacy. Though Thoreau's voice was his own — sharper, more ascetic, more rooted in practice — it was Emerson who gave him the courage to trust his path. Without Emerson's encouragement, there might never have been *Walden,* that great scripture of simplicity and conscience. Thoreau's resistance to unjust laws, his willingness to go to jail rather than support slavery, his radical fidelity to principle, all bore the mark of Emerson's teaching that the individual must follow conscience even against the state. Together, Emerson and Thoreau formed the twin pillars of Transcendentalism, one expansive, the other uncompromising, both shaping American ideals of independence and integrity.

Beyond his immediate circle, Emerson's influence seeped into the veins of American philosophy. The pragmatists — William James, John Dewey, Charles Sanders Peirce — found in him a precursor. His insistence that truth is not static but unfolding, that ideas are provisional, that life is a circle of continual expansion, resonated with their sense of thought as experiment. James in particular admired Emerson, calling him "the philosopher of the moral life." The American tradition of philosophy as practical, experiential, open-ended owes much to the seeds planted by Emerson.

In poetry, his spirit echoed through Emily Dickinson, who kept his works in her library and whose compressed, enigmatic verse shares kinship with his aphoristic sentences. Robert Frost, too, carried forward Emerson's reverence for nature as teacher, his blending of plain speech with metaphysical depth. And later still, T. S. Eliot, though critical of Transcendentalism, was shaped by its atmosphere, its insistence that the poet is a seer.

In politics and social thought, Emerson's legacy is equally profound. His words on self-reliance and conscience inspired reformers, abolitionists, suffragists. His defense of the dignity of every soul became part of the moral vocabulary of American democracy. Martin Luther King Jr., in his own cadences of justice, echoed Emerson's conviction that conscience must stand against unjust law, that the soul is sovereign, that freedom is not granted but inherent. Gandhi, too, read Emerson, finding in his call to self-reliance a resonance with the Indian tradition of swaraj — self-rule, beginning with the individual.

In spirituality, Emerson opened doors that remain wide. His engagement with Eastern texts — the Bhagavad Gita, the Upanishads, Buddhist scriptures — introduced them to American audiences at a time when such works were scarcely known. He helped seed the cross-cultural dialogue that would blossom in the twentieth century with the spread of Vedanta, Zen, and comparative mysticism. His Oversoul anticipates, in its universality, the later movements of perennial philosophy and interfaith exploration.

Even in psychology, Emerson's seeds sprouted. His vision of the self as dynamic, creative, in contact with a deeper unity, foreshadowed modern ideas of the unconscious, of human potential, of transpersonal awareness. Carl Jung, though rooted in European soil, spoke of archetypes and collective unconscious in ways that echo Emerson's Oversoul. Humanistic psychologists of the twentieth century — Maslow, Rogers — drew on the same conviction that each person carries within a spark of transcendence.

But Emerson's legacy is not confined to named influences. It lies also in the atmosphere of American culture: the valorization of the individual, the celebration of nature, the suspicion of conformity, the reverence for fresh speech. Every time an American voice insists on trusting its own experience, every time a poet looks to the local landscape as scripture, every time a reformer appeals to conscience above law, Emerson is there, whispering still.

And yet, his legacy is complex. Critics have noted his aloofness from the raw struggles of his time, his tendency to withdraw into serenity while others pressed into battle. Some accused him of optimism too airy, of abstraction too vague. Others found his individualism dangerous, a seed of self-absorption in a culture that could tilt toward selfishness. Such critiques are not without merit. But even here, his legacy proves fertile: he provokes debate, demands discernment, resists complacency. He is not a saint to be enshrined but a voice to be wrestled with, one who still unsettles as he inspires.

In the twentieth century, Emerson's star dimmed somewhat in academic philosophy, overshadowed by more systematic thinkers. Yet outside the academy, his words continued to circulate, quoted in speeches, etched into anthologies, read by seekers. In the twenty-first century, his relevance has grown again, as environmental thought, interspiritual dialogue, and movements for authenticity rediscover his insights. His transparent eyeball, once mocked, now seems prophetic in an age seeking ecological reverence. His call to self-reliance rings anew in a culture grappling with conformity of another sort: mass media, consumerism, digital distraction.

Ultimately, Emerson's legacy lies in his sentences. Compact, luminous, they continue to ignite thought: "Trust thyself: every heart vibrates to that iron string." "The creation of a thousand forests is in one acorn." "Nothing is at last sacred but the integrity of your own mind." These are not relics but sparks, still capable of kindling courage and wonder. Each reader, encountering them, becomes anew the friend Emerson always sought: one before whom he might think aloud, one who is invited into communion with the Oversoul.

Thus his legacy is not finished. Seeds once scattered continue to germinate. Each generation rediscovers him, each finds in him what it needs: for some, a prophet of nature; for others, a champion of individuality; for others still, a mystic of unity. Emerson is not a monument but a spring, his waters flowing as long as there are souls thirsty for truth.

## The Eternal Emerson

The life of Ralph Waldo Emerson begins in the narrow streets of Boston and ends in the quiet ridges of Concord, yet its arc extends far beyond geography. It is the story of a boy born into poverty who became the voice of a nation's spirit, of a minister who resigned his pulpit only to become a preacher to the world, of a thinker who turned from tradition to intuition and discovered in his own heart the Oversoul that binds all. To trace his journey is to trace the awakening of American thought, the moment when a young republic began to believe that its landscapes, its conscience, its individuals were sufficient ground for philosophy and poetry.

Emerson was never a system-builder. He left no Summa, no ordered structure of metaphysics, no creed to be memorized. Instead, he left sentences — sparks, fragments, shafts of light. His genius lay not in constructing systems but in igniting awakenings. He wanted not disciples but friends, not followers but individuals awakened to their own divinity. His essays are invitations rather than conclusions, beginnings rather than endings. To read him is to be summoned, to be asked: what do you see? what truth whispers in your own breast? what horizon calls you beyond the circle you now inhabit?

And yet, though fragmentary, his vision coheres. Nature, self-reliance, the Oversoul, friendship, beauty, love, circles, poetry, politics of conscience — all are facets of one truth: that the divine is present here and now, in every soul, in every leaf, in every act of fidelity. Life is revelation, if only we will see. Trusting that revelation requires courage, for society conspires against individuality, custom dulls perception, grief clouds vision. But the courage to trust, to perceive freshly, to act from conscience, opens the soul to freedom. This is Emerson's central gift: not doctrines to repeat but freedom to live.

The trials he endured — the deaths of father, wife, brothers, child; the loneliness of resignation; the faltering of memory — gave depth to his serenity. He did not speak from untested optimism but from sorrow transfigured. When he urged self-reliance, it was the counsel of one who had stood alone. When he proclaimed the Oversoul, it was the testimony of one who had felt unity in the midst of grief. When he celebrated circles of becoming, it was the wisdom of one who had lived endings that became beginnings. His philosophy is not a denial of suffering but a way through it.

In Concord, among orchards and rivers, he lived simply, his house a place of books and conversation, his life a rhythm of walks, lectures, and writing. Visitors found him both accessible and elusive: a man of gentle courtesy, yet also of inward distance, as if part of him always listened to a silence beyond. He belonged to his town, yet he also belonged to no place, for his mind moved in universals. He was, as Carlyle called him, "a new kind of man," embodying both Yankee plainness and mystical depth.

What remains of Emerson is not only history but presence. His words continue to vibrate because they touch perennial truths: the sovereignty of conscience, the sanctity of nature, the unity of being, the endlessness of growth. These truths cannot be exhausted by time, for they are woven into the fabric of existence itself. Each generation rediscovers them, whether in movements for justice, in poetry of the land, in quests for authenticity, in dialogues between cultures. Emerson is eternal not because he escapes history but because he speaks to the eternal within history.

To stand at his grave in Sleepy Hollow is to feel this paradox. The stone is simple, weathered, set among pines and birches. Visitors leave flowers, stones, notes. Around him lie Thoreau, Hawthorne, the Alcotts — the Concord circle reunited in silence. And yet, Emerson is not contained there. He walks still in every forest where someone feels awe, speaks still in every conscience that resists conformity, breathes still in every word spoken freshly. The transparent eyeball did not vanish with his body; it became the symbol of a way of seeing always available.

Perhaps the truest tribute to Emerson is not to admire him but to practice what he taught: to trust oneself, to see freshly, to live in harmony with nature, to act from conscience, to honor friendship, to cherish beauty, to accept grief as teacher, to welcome circles of becoming. His wisdom is not behind us but before us, waiting to be embodied in each life. He is not to be enshrined but to be continued.

Thus the eternal Emerson is not a man of the nineteenth century only, nor merely the Sage of Concord, but the voice of the Oversoul reminding us still: life is divine, now; you are part of the whole; trust the inner light; live in the radiance of the present. His sentences remain seeds. The soil is always ready. The harvest is always beginning.

## Glossary of Key Terms

This glossary gathers Emerson's key ideas and the living vocabulary of Transcendentalism as they appear throughout *The Wisdom of Ralph Waldo Emerson: Nature, Self-Reliance, and the Oversoul.* Each entry is concise yet contemplative, written to clarify meaning without draining the words of their light.

**Abolition.** More than a political platform in Emerson's usage: a moral imperative born of the soul's recognition that every person bears divinity. To resist slavery was to honor the Oversoul in all.

**Absolute.** Emerson's name for the unconditioned ground of being—often intimated as "the One," "the Eternal," or "the Whole"—which time, circumstance, and language can only suggest, never contain.

**American Scholar (The).** Emerson's figure for the liberated mind in a new nation: one who learns first from Nature, next from the past, and finally from action—speaking freshly rather than echoing Europe.

**Analogy / Correspondence.** The doctrine that natural facts mirror spiritual facts. Rivers, stones, seasons, the flight of birds—each is emblematic, each a parable the soul can read.

**Beauty.** Not ornament but revelation: the form in which spirit shines through matter. When proportion, vitality, and meaning cohere, the world discloses its radiance.

**Character.** The moral shape of a life. For Emerson, character outweighs talent; it is the slow, luminous crystallization of conscience into conduct.

**Circles.** Emerson's image of endless becoming: every horizon is provisional, every conviction a circumference awaiting a greater center. Wisdom lives by enlargement, not by fixity.

**Commodity.** The first use of Nature—its practical service to human life. Emerson acknowledges it, then urges us beyond utility toward Beauty, Language, Discipline, and Spirit.

**Concord.** A place and a symbol: the small New England town where orchards, river, and common life became a scripture. Concord names the harmony between locality and universality.

**Conscience.** The inner lawgiver. Not merely feeling, but the Oversoul's pressure within the breast; fidelity to it is the root of self-reliance and civil courage.

**Conduct of Life (The).** Emerson's mature inquiry into power, wealth, culture, behavior, worship, beauty, illusions. A manual of spiritual pragmatics: how to carry the soul's light through the day.

**Compensation.** The hidden justice woven into existence: gains and losses, joys and griefs, balancing like a great ledger in the moral universe. Not fatalism, but law.

**Divinity School Address (1838).** The soft-spoken thunderclap: Emerson's declaration that revelation is immediate, that Christ is exemplar not exception, that the soul's intuition outruns ritual.

**Ecstasy / Rapture.** The heightened state in which separateness falls away and "wise silence" floods perception. Emerson's transparent clarity rather than frenzy—a lucidity that feels like dawn.

**Emersonian Idealism.** A lived insight, not a system: spirit precedes form; mind reads world because mind and world share one source. The real is a wedding of soul and fact.

**Experience.** Both a late essay and a condition. After grief, Emerson discovers the opacity of life—yet presses for a second, deeper seeing that turns fate into opening.

**Fate.** The mesh of limits—body, history, temperament. Emerson neither denies nor worships it; he yokes fate to freedom by character and insight.

**Freedom.** The soul's consent to its own highest law. Not caprice, but obedience to the inner light that alone can transfigure circumstance.

**Friendship.** Communion without possession: the miracle of being known and allowed to be. A sacrament of the Oversoul refracted between two.

**Genius.** That in each person which is most original and therefore most universal. Genius trusts its vision before it can prove it.

**Immanence / Transcendence.** Emerson holds both: the divine suffuses leaves and lenses every moment (immanence), yet ever exceeds our grasp (transcendence).

**Intuition.** Primary knowing. Earlier than inference, deeper than opinion—the Oversoul's hint within. Reason in Coleridge's sense, not mere ratiocination.

**Language.** "Fossil poetry." Words begin as vivid contact with things and harden over time. The poet's work is to thaw them back into fire.

**Law (Moral / Natural).** One current, two faces. The grain of the world and the grain of the soul run together; to move with that grain is virtue.

**Metre-Making Argument.** Emerson's claim in *The Poet* that poetry comes first, the proof follows—the imagination sets the form and gives measure to meaning.

**Nature.** Emerson's master-word. More than scenery: the living garment of God, a five-fold scripture—Commodity, Beauty, Language, Discipline, Spirit—through which the soul awakens.

**Nonconformity.** The refusal to trade truth for approval. Not mere contrariness, but the negative space that protects the positive work of fidelity.

**Original Relation to the Universe.** Emerson's summons to first-hand life: meet the world without interposed authorities; receive from the root, not only the branch.

**Oversoul (The).** The universal life, the wise silence, the "eternal One" in which all persons partake. Unity without erasure; the sea of which each soul is a wave.

**Perception.** A moral as well as optical act. We see by what we are; to cleanse the heart is to clarify the eye.

**Poet (The).** Not a job but a vocation: the representative human who names freshly, restores the world's firstness, and lets spirit blaze through speech.

**Pragmatic Seed.** Emerson's sense that truth proves itself in life, in conduct and consequence—an intuition that will flower in American pragmatism.

**Providence.** The benevolent curvature of reality discerned over time. Distinct from passivity; it asks our cooperation to complete its arc.

**Reason vs. Understanding.** Following Coleridge: *Reason* as intuitive insight, *Understanding* as analytic skill. Emerson prizes their union, but crowns Reason.

**Representative Men.** Portraits of human possibilities—Plato, Shakespeare, Montaigne, Napoleon, Goethe—used not to enthrone heroes but to awaken correspondences in the reader.

**Self-Reliance.** The courage to obey the inner law even at the cost of favor. Self here means soul, not ego: reliance is consent to the divine within.

**Society.** Useful but hazardous: a conspiracy toward conformity. Emerson honors community best by protecting the individual flame that, paradoxically, illumines all.

**Solitude.** The workshop of truth. Not misanthropy but the interval in which the soul can hear what the crowd drowns.

**Spirit.** The life-breath of things; what thinks through us, grows the tree, and binds the stars. Often synonymous with Oversoul, but felt as presence.

**Sublime.** The shock of disproportion that enlarges us—vast sky, ocean swell, moral heroism—where fear and joy marry into awe.

**Symbol / Emblem.** The natural fact shimmering with more-than-literal meaning. Emerson reads world as scripture: twig as text, thunder as commentary.

**Transparent Eyeball (The).** Emerson's emblem of egoless seeing: self becomes aperture, world rushes in, and "I am part or particle of God."

**Trust.** The soul's yes to its own best perception. Emerson's quiet heroism: act while the light is in you.

**Unity.** The hidden consonance beneath multiplicity; the music we half-remember and wholly seek. Ethics and aesthetics flow from this oneness.

**Walden.** Thoreau's embodiment of Emersonian principles: simplicity, conscience, intimacy with nature. A neighboring star in the same constellation.

**Woman in the Nineteenth Century.** Margaret Fuller's Transcendentalist expansion of Emersonian liberty into the emancipation of women; self-reliance made social.

**Wordsworth / Carlyle (Influences).** Wordsworth: the sanctity of the common; Carlyle: the gravity of character and history. Emerson converses, then carves his own path.

**Yielding (Spiritual).** The paradox of power: not passive collapse but supple obedience to the grain of the world—water's strength, sap's ascent.

**Zeal (Religious).** Emerson's cautionary word: heat without light. He seeks the reverse—light that warms, conviction without cruelty.

**American Scripture.** Nature read as sacred text in a new land; rivers as psalms, pines as pillars, starlight as marginalia.

**Apprenticeship to Truth.** A lifelong pedagogy: each insight a lesson, each loss a teacher, each circle the next grade of freedom.

**The Conduct of Worship.** Not ceremony alone but a life aligned; reverence woven through errands, gardens, friendships, justice.

**Discipline (of Nature).** Nature trains the soul: cold instructs, labor steadies, limits teach form—beauty with backbone.

**Temporality / Eternity.** Time as the moving edge of the timeless. Emerson reads each hour as a window into the Whole.

**Originality.** Faithfulness to one's present vision even against one's past sentences. The soul must not live off yesterday's bread.

**The Scholar's Duty.** To be a *one-man university*: reader of nature, steward of books, maker of action—translating insight into life.

**Justice.** The practical name of unity in public. When the Oversoul enters history, it appears as conscience turned policy.

**Sermon vs. Life.** Emerson's transposition: the sermon is the life. Words matter when they are the echo of being.

**Nature's Five Uses.** Commodity, Beauty, Language, Discipline, Spirit: ascending rungs by which perception climbs toward praise.

**Power.** Not domination, but the capacity to carry vision into deed. For Emerson, power is moral voltage—character conducting truth.

**Wealth.** A tool, not a telos. Its right measure is the enlargement of mind and the liberation of time for inward and outward service.

**Worship.** Attention enthroned. Wherever the eye becomes transparent and the heart consenting, worship occurs—field, study, street alike.

**Youth.** The perennial metaphor of Emerson's hope: not an age but a spirit of firstness that any soul can reclaim.

**Zest.** Emerson's worldly sacrament: to take the day as given, and give oneself wholly to it, until it yields its hidden wine.

Made in the USA
Middletown, DE
04 February 2026

28066465R00086